GHOSTLY
COUNTY DURHAM

ROB KIRKUP

FOREWORD BY DARREN W. RITSON

In memory of my uncle, Steve Addison,

who passed away in August 2009

First published 2010

The History Press
The Mill, Brimscombe Port
Stroud, Gloucestershire, GL5 2QG
www.thehistorypress.co.uk

British Library Cataloguing in Publication Data.
A catalogue record for this book is available from the British Library.

ISBN 978 0 7509 5124 1

Typesetting and origination by The History Press
Printed in Great Britain

Contents

Foreword

I have been acquainted with Rob Kirkup for a few years now for we both share a passion: ghost hunting. Like most people, we each live a fairly mundane existence, doing our own thing, yet slowly and positively plodding on with everyday life, dealing with what trials and tribulations it decides to throws at us. Unlike most people, however, both Rob and I track down ghosts, interview those who have seen or felt them, and write up the accounts for future generations to read about.

In August 2009 I had the pleasure of meeting Rob for the first time as we were both taking part in a book signing at Waterstone's in Newcastle-upon-Tyne. Rob was promoting his second book *Ghostly Tyne & Wear* and I was promoting my newly released *Haunted Newcastle* – both volumes which are cram-packed with nail-biting narratives of ghosts and ghouls and things that go 'bump' in the night. I knew straight away that I had met a man with a great passion and a deep desire for investigating the paranormal. Rob is a man after my own heart; his tenaciousness and his will to succeed in his endeavours are second to none. He has found himself an interest and has turned it into something really positive. Unlike most, he has got up off his backside and decided to do something with his passion, and for this he must be congratulated. Writing books and ghost hunting takes up a serious amount of time and calls for utmost dedication and total discipline.

Ghosts are fascinating, don't you think? The idea of someone or something permanently leaving its mark upon the atmosphere for you get a glimpse of when the time, or perhaps when the conditions are right, and just when you least expect it, is an extraordinary concept to say the least … yet it happens. The idea of the soul or spirit of a deceased individual coming back from the dead to wreak vengeance or havoc on a wrong-doer, or to perhaps right a wrong in some way is incredible … yet reports keep coming in to suggest that it does happen. Ghosts are indeed a magical aspect of our heritage and stories of such denizens date back many thousands of years.

Indeed, the tradition of telling ghost stories round a camp fire on a dark Halloween night, or perhaps sitting round a lit candle on Christmas Eve awaiting '12 bells' also goes back many a year and I believe this is a tradition, or an aspect of our lives that should live on forever. I am sure, with books like this one, the tradition of the classic ghost story will indeed survive for many years yet.

This is the third book in Rob's fantastic series of 'Ghostly' tomes and I am so happy to have been able to pen this foreword. His first two books covered the counties that are Northumberland, and Tyne & Wear. Where better to concentrate on next, than the beautiful and historic county that is Durham. It is a rich and varied region of the north-east of England and with its many ancient castles, hotels, pubs and inns, battlefields and other places of historical interest, this book does not disappoint. One of my best ghost sightings happened in County Durham and the full story of what transpired is featured herein. I will not give too many details away, other than say it was spine-chilling to say the least, and it was a defining moment in my life and in my career as a ghost hunter and paranormal investigator.

For the thrill-seeking ghost enthusiast I would recommend an organised 'fright night', which are full of gimmicks and scares around every corner, or indeed one of the wide variety of television programmes on the subject. For the more serious student of psychic study and ghostlore, I give you *Ghostly County Durham*.

You, the reader, have made a good choice. Your decision to choose *Ghostly County Durham* will most certainly improve your understanding of not only the tremendous yet terrifying haunting aspects of the region, but you will soon know how to report, write up and document for yourself, genuine accounts of paranormal activity from our historical and most haunted heritage.

Darren W. Ritson, 2010
Author and Ghost Hunter

Acknowledgements

I'd like to begin by expressing my gratitude to my family for their support throughout the writing of *Ghostly County Durham*; especially my wife Jo, my parents Tom and Emily, and my brother Thomas. I would also like to thank my in-laws Michael and Patricia, my brother-in-law, James, and Jo's grandparents Norman and Margaret.

Many thanks go to John Crozier, Andrew Markwell, and David Henderson for accompanying me on literally dozens of 'road trips' to the locations you will read about throughout this book, conducting research and taking the photographs that you see on these pages.

My close friends have offered no end of encouragement during this project and I would like to thank them all. In particular John Gray, Dan Armstrong, Harry Dalton, Ryan Elwell, Brian Moore, Peter Slater, Andrew Davidson, Paul Morton, Richard Stokoe, and Paul Bicker.

I was thrilled when Darren Ritson agreed to write the foreword for *Ghostly County Durham*. I have immersed myself in many of his books over the last few years, and it was great to finally meet him last summer. I was immediately impressed by his knowledge and the enthusiasm that he has on the subject of the supernatural. We have gone on to become good friends, and I've no doubt in my mind that his career as an author will continue to go from strength to strength. Thanks Darren.

I am indebted to the staff and owners of the locations included in this book; they could not have been more helpful. I am grateful to them all for allowing their properties' inclusion in this book.

A number of people were kind enough to talk to me about their personal ghostly experiences. I would like to extend my gratitude to them all; Carol Bowen, Jonathan Horner, Mark Smith, Maggie Bell, Jay Brown, Andrew Marsay, Claire Robinson, Dean Maynard, Lee Foster, and David Butler.

Last, but by no means least, I would like to thank everyone at the History Press, Matilda Richards and Beth Amphlett in particular, for the faith they have showed in me throughout the 'Ghostly' series, and their support and guidance in the writing of *Ghostly County Durham*.

'The Journey' by Fenwick Lawson. This bronze statue stands in Durham's Millennium Square and pays tribute to the story of St Cuthbert's coffin.

Introduction

There is archaeological evidence of settlements within the area of County Durham dating back to 2000 BC. However, the present City of Durham, and the county that has grown around it, dates from AD 995, when monks from Lindisfarne settled on what was then known as Dunholme as the final resting place of the remains of St Cuthbert.

One-hundred-and-twenty years previously, in 875, Danish fleets were relentlessly invading England, and the holy island of Lindisfarne was at risk of being completely destroyed. The monks decided they had no choice but to leave the island. They gathered up their most sacred relics – The Lindisfarne Gospels, remains of King Oswald and St Aidan, and the coffin of St Cuthbert – and set out on a journey which would take them to Chester-le-Street, and eventually lead them to Durham.

During the medieval period the city found spiritual prominence and became the most important religious site in England, due to the remains of St Cuthbert being situated behind the High Altar of Durham Cathedral. It was claimed that the miraculous healing powers St Cuthbert had had in life had extended to death, as visitors to his shrine were said to be have been cured of all manner of diseases.

In the present day, the City of Durham is a wonderfully historic location with 569 listed buildings within the city centre. It is famed for the magnificent castle and cathedral, which both date back almost 1,000 years and are jointly designated a UNESCO World Heritage Site. However, during the Second World War the city became a target for German bombers, and it is said that on one occasion many of these landmarks would have been lost had it not been for the timely intervention of St Cuthbert working one of his miracles. In the early hours of 1 May 1942 the city of Durham was awoken by an air-raid siren and the sound of Junkers and Dornier bombers in the distance nearing Durham. The previous week had seen bombs drop on Exeter, Bath, Norwich, and York, and it had been feared that Durham would be next. The night's sky was clear and a full moon illuminated the cathedral, making it an easy target for the enemy. However, as the ominous drone of the bombers grew louder as they neared their target, a dense white mist suddenly began to rise and completely engulfed most of the city centre, including the castle and cathedral, hiding them from view. The aircraft circled for almost an hour, until they gave up and headed east towards the coast, leaving the City of Durham unscathed.

Witnesses have said that the mist appeared so suddenly, and so timely, that they thought it must have been a deliberate smokescreen. One woman said, 'Truly, I saw the hand of God'. The all clear sounded at 4.02 a.m., and with that the mist dispersed completely, leaving the City of Durham bathed in brilliant moonlight.

This was not the first time that the spirit of St Cuthbert had intervened to attempt to assist Durham in times of war; The monk Symeon of Durham wrote over nine centuries ago of St Cuthbert bringing forth a similar mist, shrouding the city when Durham came under threat from William the Conqueror.

These are just two astounding stories that have touched the history of the city, and county, of Durham. Over the centuries the people of County Durham have witnessed some incredible, and on other occasions horrific, occurrences. Throughout the pages of this book you will read of many of these happenings, including torture, plague, and cold-blooded murder, and how they have contributed to County Durham being one of the most haunted counties in the UK.

So sit back, dim the lights, and allow me to be your guide on a terrifying spectral journey across Ghostly County Durham.

The photographs throughout this book are the author's own, unless otherwise stated.

Rob Kirkup, 2010

A-Z of Haunted Locations
in County Durham

Durham Castle by moonlight. (By kind permission of Durham University)

Ancient Unicorn Inn

The village of Bowes is situated in the North Pennines, an Area of Outstanding Natural Beauty. It was built around the Roman fort of Lavatrae, and later the Norman castle of Bowes. At the heart of the village is the Ancient Unicorn Inn, a sixteenth-century coaching inn steeped in history.

A number of eminent guests have stayed at the Ancient Unicorn, the most famous being Charles Dickens who stayed at the inn in early 1838 while researching his third novel, *Nicholas Nickelby*. He had heard rumours of the cruelty that occurred in northern boarding schools, and in the form of the nearby Bowes Academy, Dickens found his inspiration for Dotheboys Hall, the fictional boarding school where unwanted children were placed in the care of the wicked one-eyed schoolmaster Wackford Squeers.

Dickens spoke to the locals about conditions at Bowes Academy, run by William Shaw, and was told that Shaw was regularly fined for mistreating boys. In the local Church of St Giles he found the graves of several pupils who had died whilst attending Bowes Academy. Amongst them, on the north side of the chancel, was the grave of George Ashton Taylor who had died aged nineteen in 1822. Dickens based the character of Smike on Taylor, later writing in a letter to a friend, 'I think his ghost put Smike into my mind on the spot.'

The Ancient Unicorn Inn's best known ghost is that of a young lady known as Emma. In life, Emma's real name was Martha Railton and in 1713 she fell in love with a local man called Roger Wrightson. They were both in their late teens and the children of rival landlords in the village. Martha's parents had the Ancient Unicorn, known at the time as the George, and Roger's parents ran the King's Head, which has long since gone. The Wrightsons were a wealthy family, and Roger's father, a hard old man also called Roger, expected his son to marry suitably well. Roger knew his father would vehemently disapprove of the relationship and so Martha and Roger had to meet in secret, often on the moorland. After one late meeting in particularly stormy weather, Roger came down with a serious fever. Four days later, on the last day of his illness, he asked to see his true love; his parents agreed and Martha came to the King's Head. However, Roger's sister, Hannah, was horrified at the thought of this relationship and refused to allow Martha access to see Roger. As Martha headed home in floods of tears, she heard the bell toll out for his

The Ancient Unicorn Inn. (By kind permission of the Ancient Unicorn Inn)

The dark-haired man has been seen standing next to this fireplace. (By kind permission of the Ancient Unicorn Inn)

departure and screamed aloud that her heart was burst. Moments later she too died. The grieving parents agreed that it had been wrong to keep Martha and Roger apart in life, so decided that they should be together in death and had them buried in one single grave at St Giles. The grave was unmarked but details of their deaths are held in the parish register.

The tragic tale was the subject of a poem by Scottish poet David Mallet, in March 1760, called 'The Ballad of Edwin and Emma', leading to Martha more commonly being referred to as Emma. Despite being laid to rest with her true love, it appears that Emma has not been able to find peace; her ghost has been seen throughout the inn on countless occasions.

On one particular instance, a visitor staying at the inn was struggling to sleep as a result of a party going on in the bar, he tried to ignore it but eventually felt the need to do something about the noise. He got dressed and headed downstairs. As he walked down through the building, the sound of music and laughter, which had been unbearably loud only a few moments earlier, seemed to fade away and he became aware of an unusual atmosphere hanging in the air. When he reached the bar the lights were off and there was silence. He struggled to find the light switch, and as his eyes slowly adapted to the darkness he realised that the bar was empty apart from a figure standing still in the middle of the room, staring directly at him. It was a young lady dressed in a green party dress. He spoke to her, but got no response. His search for the light switch became more frantic as he became unnerved, as she appeared to watch him feel his way along the wall. He finally found the switch and as he turned the light on the woman vanished before his very eyes.

Emma is not the only spirit that haunts the Ancient Unicorn Inn; a dark-haired gentleman is often seen standing next to the fireplace, a boy believed to be twelve years of age is said to haunt the cellar, and a bearded man wearing a bowler hat has been seen wandering through the inn.

Jay Brown of Northern Ghost Investigations (NGI) was part of an investigation at the Ancient Unicorn Inn in 2005, and he experienced something amazing that he still cannot rationalise to this day:

I was sat in the dining area of the Ancient Unicorn. With me were a few other members of NGI, one of whom was the team medium. As I stared lazily into the large mirror that dominated a nearby wall, the medium was talking about what he was picking up on in this room.

As he spoke, in the darkness behind where he was stood, I began to see what I can only describe as a shimmering darkness. Nothing that made me immediately shout 'ghost' – just something that caught my eye.

As my attention fixed more and more on this shimmer, it began to take a form – human shaped, behind the right shoulder of the medium. The more I watched the more the dark shimmer became a billowing brown cloud with the shape and dimensions of a 6ft tall man. I glanced once or twice over towards where the medium was stood, but nothing could be seen; it was only through the mirror that I could make out this cloud.

As I watched more, the medium then began to talk about how he sensed that there was once a fire at the Unicorn and that a couple of people had died. Once he said this, the cloud just vanished.

Later that night, I heard that a number of visitors in the past had witnessed strange events in this mirror. I don't know whether it was just my eyes playing tricks on me that night – the room was lit by candles which were dancing shadows around the walls of the dining room, but afterwards it did seem strange that I'd witnessed this smoky cloud behind the medium and then, in the moments afterwards, he began to talk about a fire and the people who had died in agony as they were consumed within it.

Visitor Information

Address:
Ancient Unicorn Inn
Bowes
Barnard Castle
County Durham
DL12 9HL

Tel: 01833 628321
Email: ancient.unicorn@virgin.net
Website: www.ancient-unicorn.com

Opening Hours:
Food served Monday – Sunday 12 noon – 2 p.m.
Monday and Sunday 7 p.m. – 9 p.m.
Tuesday – Saturday 6 p.m. – 9.30 p.m.

How to Get There: The Ancient Unicorn Inn is situated on the main street in Bowes
OS Map Reference: NY 995 135

Additional Information:
- The bar sells a variety of quality real ales, beer and cider, as well as wine by the glass or the bottle, and soft drinks
- You can enjoy a bar meal from a menu of delicious home-cooked food made with fresh, seasonal local produce, or opt for a meal in the candle-lit restaurant where you can choose from the range of daily changing regional specialities, the *à la carte* menu or the mouth-watering vegetarian options. Details of the menu can be found on the website
- The Ancient Unicorn Inn offers travellers cosy, newly re-furbished bedrooms, all *en-suite*, with tea and coffee-making facilities and a television. Some courtyard rooms have Freeview channels. For details of booking and prices please visit the website
- The Ancient Unicorn can host parties or events, catering for buffets for up to 120 people and for more formal occasions for up to forty people

Barnard Castle

*B*arnard Castle stands in the town of the same name, situated on a cliff top overlooking the River Tees. The foundation of the castle dates back to the early twelfth-century when Guy de Baliol, who had came to England as part of William the Conqueror's invading army, built a timber castle, choosing this site due to the strategic position the castle would command; defended by the river on one side and steep cliffs on another.

In 1125, Guy's nephew, Bernard de Baliol, began work on rebuilding the castle in stone and enlarged the site protecting it with a surrounding curtain wall. The castle, and the town which rapidly developed around it, took its name from the man who had overseen the building of the stone fortress – 'Bernard's Castle'.

In 1138, Bernard fought at the Battle of the Standard on Cowton Moor near Northallerton, in which English forces repelled a Scottish Army led by King David I. Bernard died in 1155 and was succeeded by his eldest son, Guy. Guy held the lands around Barnard Castle for only seven years before his death in 1162. The estate passed into the hands of his brother, Bernard de Baliol II, until his death in 1199. He left no male heir and as a result the castle was passed down to his cousin, Eustace de Helicourt, who changed his name to Baliol upon his succession.

In 1216, Hugh de Baliol was a close ally of King John and helped to defend the North against a revolt from the Northumbrian Barons, supported by Alexander I of Scotland. The castle was unsuccessfully besieged in July of that year and King Alexander's brother-in-law, Eustace de Vesci, lost his life during the siege; whilst riding around the castle he was hit in the forehead by a crossbow bolt, which killed him instantly.

Hugh died in 1228 and his son, John de Baliol, succeeded him, going on to become arguably the most powerful member of the family. He was wed to Devorguilla of Galloway (who was aged just thirteen at the time) in 1223, marrying into a noble family descended from kings of Scotland. Upon the death of her father, Alan, Lord of Galloway, in 1234 the couple acquired land and titles, becoming one of the wealthiest families in Britain. In order to protect his land, John callously held his wife's illegitimate brother prisoner at Barnard Castle from 1235 to 1296.

When John died in 1269, Devorguilla had his heart embalmed and placed inside a silver casket which travelled with her always. In April 1273 she founded a Cistercian

Barnard Castle. (By kind permission of English Heritage)

Abbey near Dumfries in his memory. Devorguilla died in 1290 and was buried at the abbey alongside John's heart. The monks at the abbey renamed it Sweetheart Abbey, the name by which it is still known today, in tribute to her.

The couple left three sons, the youngest son, John de Baliol II, became King of Scotland in 1290, but war broke out six years later and John surrendered his throne and was taken to the Tower of London, where he was held prisoner, and all of his English properties, including Barnard Castle, were seized by the Crown.

The king granted the castle to Guy de Beauchamp, Earl of Warwick, in 1307 and the estate stayed in the Beauchamp family until 1446, when Henry Beauchamp died without a male heir. It passed into the hands of his sister Anne, who had married Richard Neville, eldest son of Richard Neville, Earl of Salisbury, in 1436.

Richard Neville gained the title of 16th Earl of Warwick and is best known in history as 'the Kingmaker', due to him being instrumental in the deposition of two kings during the War of the Roses. Richard was defeated and killed by King Edward IV at the Battle of Barnet on the 14 April 1471 and his widow, Anne, was completely overlooked as the lordship, and her estates, were handed to Anne's son-in-law, Richard, Duke of Gloucester, who was to become King Richard III in 1483.

Richard had great plans for improvements and expansion of Barnard Castle, but he was killed at Bosworth Field in 1485 before his alterations were realised.

Visitors to the Round Tower have experienced the feeling of being followed.
(By kind permission of English Heritage)

The castle was handed back to Anne Neville who then granted all of her estates to King Henry VII, on the understanding that they would be returned to her family after her death. This was never carried out and Barnard Castle was held by the Crown for over a century until 1603, during which time the castle fell into decline and was in desperate need of repair.

In 1536, Barnard Castle was besieged by rebels unhappy with the new Protestant religion. The Constable of Barnard, Robert Bowes, was forced to surrender the castle due to many of his own men sympathising with the rebels and therefore being considered untrustworthy. The leader of the rebels was arrested and hanged the following year.

The Rising of the North, a plot devised at nearby Raby Castle to depose Queen Elizabeth I and have her replaced by Mary, Queen of Scots, threatened the castle in 1569. Sir George Bowes was loyal to Elizabeth and went to Barnard Castle preparing it for inevitable attack and stocking it with provisions and men. Over 5,000 rebels appeared at the castle on 2 December 1569 and the castle was besieged for eleven days and nights. By 12 December things were looking bleak for the defenders. A couple of days earlier the Outer Ward had been breached in two places, leading Bowes and his men to retreat into the Inner Ward. The attackers had also cut off the supply of water into the castle. Due to this, over 200 of the soldiers chose to leap from the castle and run for their lives, rather than die fighting at Barnard Castle. Many of these soldiers broke their legs, arms, and even necks, on landing and were quickly disposed of by the enemy. On the eleventh day, 13 December, Sir George surrendered and marched out of the castle with over 300 of his loyal soldiers. The castle was lost to the rebels, but the delay forced by Sir George and his men bought the Crown time to muster their troops and the rebellion was defeated.

In 1603 King James I granted the castle to the Earl of Somerset, Robert Carr. It was transferred to the Prince of Wales in 1615, and in turn sold to the City of London in 1626.

Sir Henry Vane bought Barnard Castle in 1630. However, he also owned Raby Castle, which is where he spent most of his time. As a result, he removed much of the stonework from Barnard Castle to make improvements at Raby, causing further disrepair and ruin to Barnard Castle. By 1636 the land inside Barnard Castle walls was being used to grow hay and at the end of the eighteenth century the castle was a hollow shell.

By 1952, Lord Barnard of Raby held the estate and placed Barnard Castle in the ownership of the Ministry of Works and it is now maintained and cared for by English Heritage.

Barnard Castle's best known ghost is that of a woman that mediums have claimed is called Lady Ann Day. Little is known of Lady Ann Day, except that she lived during the sixteenth century and was murdered at the castle while still relatively young. She was thrown to her death from the castle wall into the Tees below. Her murderer's name is lost to history. Hundreds of horrified visitors to the castle have witnessed a young woman, dressed all in white, fall from the castle; some have claimed the fall is accompanied by her scream, but just as the woman appears to hit the water there is no splash, it's as if she just vanishes.

Many visitors to the castle have experienced an uneasy feeling in the Round Tower; some have described it as the sense that someone is following them. However, as soon as they leave the tower the feeling lifts.

Visitors to the town of Barnard Castle would be advised to keep one eye on the skies above the town as there has been a large number of UFO sightings reported over the last century. The most extraordinary report was from the night of 6 June 1977. A motorcyclist saw a low-flying saucer-shaped glowing object overhead. It stopped directly above him and he felt it giving off extreme heat. It seemed to be draining power from his engine as his motorcycle spluttered to a halt and would not restart. The craft then took off at high speed and he lost sight of it moments later.

The Undercroft beneath the Round Tower. (By kind permission of English Heritage)

Visitor Information

Address:
Barnard Castle
Durham
DL12 8PR

Tel: 01833 638212
Website: www.english-heritage.org.uk

Opening Hours:
April – September, open seven days a week 10 a.m. – 6 p.m.
October – November, open seven days a week 10 a.m. – 4 p.m.
November – March, open Thursday – Monday 10 a.m. – 4 p.m.
Closed 24 – 26 December and 1 January

How to Get There: Barnard Castle is located 25 miles south west of the City of Durham. It is accessible from most directions: the A688 from the north, A1 from the south, and on the A66 from the east and the west
OS Map Reference: NZ 055 165

Additional Information:
- Barnard Castle is suitable for people in wheelchairs
- Dogs are allowed on leads
- There is a shop at the castle which sells guidebooks, gifts, and refreshments
- There is a picnic area
- There are toilets at the castle

Beamish Hall

*I*n 1268 Philip de la Leigh gave his daughter and Sir Bertram Monboucher the manor at Tanfield as a wedding dowry. In the years that followed, Sir Bertram built the first manor for his family on the site upon which Beamish Hall now stands. Five generations of Monbouchers lived at Beamish Manor before the final family member died in 1400.

Throughout the Middle Ages, the estate was owned by various local aristocrats, including the famous Northumbrian Percy family. In 1569 the manor of Beamish was forfeited to the Crown due to the involvement of Thomas Percy, 7th Earl of Northumberland, in the 'Rising of the North'. After the rebellion failed, Thomas fled to Scotland, but was captured by the Earl of Morton, one of the leading Scottish nobles. He was held prisoner for three years before being handed over to Queen Elizabeth I in exchange for £2,000. On 22 August 1572 he was beheaded at York.

The oldest part of the present Hall dates from 1620, when a new manor house was built by the Wray family.

In 1682, Timothy Davison, a Governor of the Merchants Company of Newcastle, bought the estate. His son, William Davison, lived at the Hall with his second wife, Dulcibella. Mary, their youngest daughter, married Sir Robert Eden, 3rd Baronet of Windlestone Hall, in 1739. In the mid-eighteenth century the Edens built the present three-storey Hall to replace the manor.

In 1803 Catherine Eden married Robert Eden Duncombe Shafto of Whitworth Hall. In 1904 their grandson, Revd Slingsby Duncombe Shafto, inherited the estate and took Eden as an additional surname.

He was succeeded by Robert Shafto, but when he died in 1949 death duties of £120,000 left his heir, also called Robert, no choice but to sell the estate. He moved to the original family home of Bavington Hall.

The National Coal Board leased Beamish Hall in 1954 and used it as a regional head office. In 1966 Durham County Council bought the Hall and sub-let part of the building to Beamish Museum to house paperwork, and another section of the Hall was used as a residential music college. The Hall stood empty for a number of years until August 2000, at which point it was refurbished and opened as Beamish Hall Country House Hotel.

Beamish Hall. (By kind permission of Beamish Hall Hotel)

The best known of the Shafto family to have held the estate at Beamish was 'Bonny' Bobby Shafto. Bobby's main residence was Whitworth Hall, but he did spend time at Beamish. It was while at Beamish Hall in the late 1770s that he met and fell in love with Bridget Bellasyse of Brancepeth. They made a handsome couple and it was not long before there was talk of a wedding. However, Bobby had always wanted to travel, so an agreement was made: Bobby would have his great adventure upon the high seas, experiencing exotic lands, but he would return home to his beloved Bridget and they would be wed and begin a family.

On the day he sailed out of the River Wear, Bridget struggled to hold back the tears as she waved him off. He waved back at her as the ship slowly headed out to sea. They continued to wave until they could no longer see one another. It has been said, although there is no historical proof, that Bridget actually wrote the popular northern rhyme that has ensured that Bobby Shafto remains a household name in the region.

> Bobby Shafto's gone to sea,
> Silver buckles at his knee;
> He'll come back and marry me,
> Bonny Bobby Shafto.
>
> Bobby Shafto's bright and fair,
> Combing down his yellow hair,
> He's my ain for ever mair,
> Bonny Bobby Shafto.
>
> Bobby Shafto's tall and slim,
> He's always dressed so neat and trim,
> The lassies they all keek at him,
> Bonny Bobby Shafto.
>
> Bobby Shafto's gett'n a bairn,
> For to dandle on his airm,
> On his airm and on his knee,
> Bobby Shafto loves me.

Bobby did return to the North East, but Bridget was never to see him again. He met another woman, Anne Duncombe, and asked for her hand in marriage. Word reached Bridget and she was devastated. She had to speak to Bobby and hear this for herself; she loved him with all her heart and was prepared to do whatever it took to win him back.

She went to Beamish Hall late one evening in the hope that he would be there, and managed to gain access at the back of Hall. As she made her way through the winding corridors she was spotted by a servant; Bridget panicked and ran down to the lower reaches of the Hall. She was worried the servant would follow her so climbed inside a casket. Unfortunately, when she closed the lid the latch fell down and she became trapped. She cried out for help, but she was in an area of the Hall that few people ever ventured. Bridget died within that casket, although no one knows if it was suffocation, thirst, or hunger that took her life.

Bobby Shafto and Anne Duncombe were married on 18 April 1774. Bobby heard rumours that Bridget had disappeared, but he would never know the truth. Bobby died in 1797, and it wasn't until the early nineteenth century, almost thirty years after she had died in such horrendous circumstances, that Bridget's mummified remains were found in the casket by a terrified cleaner. Ironically, the only other item within the casket was an old wedding dress.

Bridget's spirit haunts Beamish Hall to this day; she is known as the Grey Lady and is seen, and heard, in the lower reaches of the Hall where she lost her life. She has also been seen looking forlornly out of the window of the Bridal Suite.

The Shafto Hall. (By kind permission of Beamish Hall Hotel)

The Grey Lady is the best known of all of Beamish Hall's ghosts, but she is by no means the only spectre to walk the old hall; staff members openly admit that there are some rooms within the Hall that don't 'feel right' and they are reluctant to go into them alone, especially after dark.

The Shafto Hall is one room in particular which has brought blind terror racing to the fore; members of staff have been alone in the room when they have heard footsteps behind them. When they have turned around, the room has been empty and the footsteps immediately stop.

An old lady dressed in Edwardian clothes and a pink hat sits in the Eden Bar, and in the Eden Room a man wearing Victorian finery stares out of the window.

In the reception area a woman believed to be named Charlotte has been seen.

In the attic rooms the light fittings have been seen to spin around. This is attributed to the ghosts of two young children who are said to play there.

Not all of the ghosts at Beamish Hall are believed to be from times long past; a medium visited the Hall in 2005 and picked up on two spirits which had not been reported previously and were both fairly recent deaths; one was a lady who was married at Beamish Hall in 2001 or 2002 and has since passed away – she has returned to haunt the Hall as her wedding day was the happiest day of her life.

The other spirit is said to be that of a young man who worked at the Hall and died in a car crash on his way home from a late shift. He is said to haunt the office area.

Visitors to Beamish Hall in search of the many ghosts that haunt the estate would find a visit to nearby Beamishburn time well spent. There is a legend dating back to the seventeenth century of a young lady in her late teens who grew up in the area. A horrific tale that a number of mediums visiting the area have retold over the years. Most versions of the legend say she was called Mary, although others say Marie. She was a well mannered young lady, very family orientated, who wanted to remain pure until the day she found the man of her dreams and was married. She was very beautiful, petite, and had long red hair, and many of the men in the village tried to woo her, but she politely rejected their advances.

One night, three men were drinking in a local public house when the topic turned to Mary. All of the men had tried to charm her (unsuccessfully) and as the drink flowed and they became steadily more inebriated they all decided to go and pay Mary a visit to ask her to reconsider turning down their advances. When they arrived at Mary's home late that evening she answered the door in her night gown, and they found her to be home alone as her parents were away and would not return until the following day. They asked if they could come in, she was afraid and

The Reception Area. (By kind permission of Beamish Hall Hotel)

said no, they ignored her reply and pushed her aside. Mary was beginning to panic and asked them again to leave; they laughed and asked her what she would do if they didn't. They pushed her into a chair and she began to scream out for help – no one came.

That night all three men raped Mary. As Mary lay upon her bed crying her heart out in the torn and bloodied remains of her night gown, the men began to sober up and panic set in as they realised that Mary knew all three of them and all she had to do was tell one person and they would be arrested, and likely executed. They decided they had to take action; two of the men held her down on her bed as she struggled, the third man approached her with a razor sharp knife in his hand. When she saw it she screamed out for help in absolute terror – it would be the last noise she would ever make as the man grabbed her tongue and cut it from her mouth. She was trying to scream out in horror and agony, but no sound came forth as she choked on the blood gushing from the wound. The men knew they still had a problem, she could write down their names and they'd still be identified as her rapists; two of the men pinned her to the floor as the third beat her hands with a mallet, breaking and splintering every bone until her hands were nothing more than pulp. In one final callous act they cut out both of her eyes; this would ensure she would never be able to see them again. With this they knew no one would ever know of the evil that took place that very night and they made a hasty exit.

Mary was all alone, in terrible pain, shame, and fear. She was now blind, unable to speak, and she'd likely never be able to use her hands again.

Her parents came home and were horrified to find what had been done to their daughter; she was very ill and drifting in and out of consciousness. Over the weeks and months that followed they cared for her and nursed her back to as near full health as she was ever likely to be.

Mary loved her parents dearly, but no one would ever be brought to justice for the horror she endured and she felt that life was no longer worth living. Using one of the few senses she still possessed, her hearing, she made her way to the fast-flowing water at Beamishburn and threw herself in. Her cold, limp, lifeless body was found the following day.

After dark, visitors to the bridge on the public footpath that crosses over Beamishburn have reported seeing the ghost of a young lady with long flowing red hair floating just above the water, she holds her arms out towards them as if to show what was done to her hands. Other visitors have claimed to have heard a woman's blood-curdling scream; some witnesses have said that it appears to be coming from beneath the water.

Beamishburn; in the dead of night Mary's ghost has been seen floating just above the water.

Visitor Information

Address:
Beamish Hall Country House Hotel
Beamish
Stanley
County Durham
DH9 0YB

Tel: 01207 233733
Email: info@beamish-hall.co.uk
Website: www.beamish-hall.co.uk

How to Get There: Leave the A1(M) at Junction 63 (Chester-le-Street), and then follow the signs to Beamish Museum, which is approximately 4 miles away. As you near the museum you will see signs for Beamish Hall Country House Hotel
OS Map Reference: NZ 211 548

Additional Information:
- Beamish Hall has thirty-six *en-suite* non-smoking bedrooms that are individually decorated to reflect the character of the building. Each room is fitted with tea and coffee-making facilities, telephone, Freeview television, hairdryer, heating control, Wifi internet access, twenty-four-hour room service, and iron and ironing board. For booking information, prices, and details of special offers, please contact Beamish Hall or visit their website
- Beamish Hall caters for corporate meetings and events, team-building days, and special celebrations. Further information can be found on their website
- Beamish Hall is the perfect setting for a wedding. The grand country house and extensive grounds provide the ideal backdrop for photographs and the ambience within the Hall is grand and traditional. Brochures can be downloaded, or a paper copy can be ordered, from the website
- The Stables Pub and Brewery offers excellent food, cooked with locally sourced ingredients. Real ale is brewed on site in their own micro brewery by expert brewer John Taylor
- Beamish Wild is a newly developed Ropes Activity Course and Birds of Prey Centre located within the woodland at Beamish Hall. Guests can benefit from discounted rates into both attractions when staying at the hotel

Bowes Castle

*B*owes Castle stands on the original site of Lavatrae, a forty-four-acre fort built by the Romans in the Flavian period to protect the road across the Pennine Mountains. The fort was constructed in the first century and was occupied until the fourth century. Bowes Castle was built in 1136 as an earth and timber construction by Alan the Red, Count of Brittany, who also owned nearby Richmond Castle.

Bowes Castle has been involved in considerable conflict over the centuries and has seen an awful lot of bloodshed and death. It was besieged in 1173 by Scottish forces led by King William of Scotland. It was so badly damaged that King Henry II ordered that the castle be rebuilt in stone as a strong defensive castle designed to withstand constant Scottish raids on the North of England. This work was carried out between 1173 and 1187. The stone keep was built with three levels, surrounded by a rectangular moat. Bowes was built with no curtain walls so it is likely that it was used as a garrison post more than a residential castle.

Between 1314 and 1322, Northern England was devastated by the Scots, and Bowes Castle was reported to be in ruins by 1325. During the seventeenth century, much of the remaining stone at the castle was stripped away for use in other buildings in the area. The present ruins of the castle keep are 53ft high, and it is possible to climb up some of the inside of the keep due to part of a staircase remaining.

By the end of the fourth century the Roman occupation in England was coming to an end. The Roman garrison stationed at Lavatrae raided the local villages and stole all of their valuables, gold in particular. The furious locals retaliated and launched an attack on the fort, and despite putting up a brave fight, the garrison was quickly defeated and the Romans mercilessly slaughtered. However, the Romans had already hid the treasure and, with not a single Roman surviving, the gold has never been recovered.

On the anniversary of the massacre, the ghosts of the murdered Roman garrison are said to appear at Bowes Castle to ritually bury their stolen gold and treasure. However, those who see these spirits are said to die in mysterious circumstances before they can share the location of the buried gold.

Visitors to Bowes have often reported a feeling of panic and fear while within the keep, sometimes accompanied by the sensation of someone standing directly behind them. Upon turning around there is no one there.

Bowes Castle. (By kind permission of English Heritage)

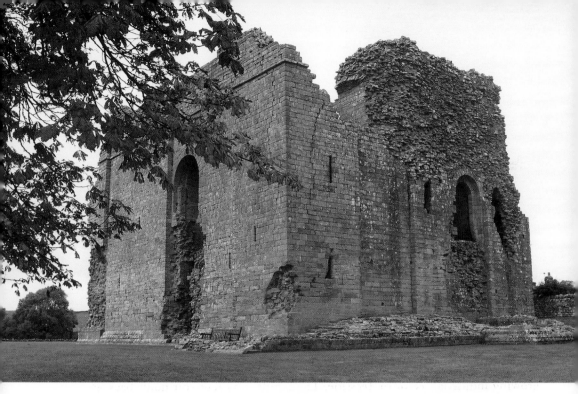

The hollow shell of Bowes Castle Keep. (By kind permission of English Heritage)

Visitor Information

Address:
Bowes Castle
Bowes
Durham
DL12 9HP

Website: www.english-heritage.org.uk

Opening Hours:
Open all year, daily, at any reasonable time

How to Get There: In Bowes village off the A66, 4 miles west of Barnard Castle town
OS Map Reference: NY 992 135

Additional Information:
- Dogs are allowed at Bowes Castle if kept on a lead
- There are no facilities at the castle
- The stonework can be uneven so please be careful during your visit

Cauldron Snout

Cauldron Snout is a waterfall on the upper reaches of the River Tees, situated below a dam at the east end of the Cow Green Reservoir. Cauldron Snout is truly a breathtaking sight, the angry water rushing, bubbling and crashing along a series of dolerite steps over 600ft long. Vertically it is 200ft from the first cataract to the last, meaning that Cauldron Snout is not only England's longest waterfall, but also the highest.

The Cow Green Reservoir was built between 1967 and 1971 to provide for the growing industrial sector of Teesside. The 2-mile long reservoir holds back 40 million cubic metres of water. The building of the reservoir was met with furious opposition from conservationists, who feared the construction of the much-needed reservoir would endanger the flora and fauna found in the Upper Teesdale area, including a number of rare plant species which had survived since the last Ice Age, such as the Blue Gentian and the Teesdale Violet. Thankfully, the construction of the reservoir didn't cause the ecological disaster feared by many, and in an effort to ensure the remaining area was not threatened by any further development, it was declared a National Nature Reserve.

The ghost of a Victorian farm girl is said to haunt Cauldron Snout. Her true identity is unknown, but she is known locally as the Singing Lady. She was in love with a married lead miner and was broken-hearted when he ended their affair. Devastated, she threw herself to the mercy of Cauldron Snout, cracked her skull on the rocks, and drowned.

Her forlorn spirit is often seen gliding across the water on moonlit nights. Witnesses have said that she appears to be crying, others say singing, but any noise she may be making is drowned out by the loud roar of the angry fast-flowing water of Cauldron Snout.

The building of the Cow Green Reservoir may not have disturbed too much of the wildlife living in the area, but it is believed that the construction of the reservoir did destroy the valley which was said to be home to Peg Powler, a green-haired, green-skinned hag from local folklore. In the eighteenth century Peg Powler was created by worried parents concerned about a number of children disappearing while near to the River Tees in the Upper Teesdale area – this was most likely due to kidnappers, or children getting too close to the perilous banks of the Tees and falling

Cauldron Snout.

Cow Green Reservoir.

into the water. Children were warned that if they went too close to the water's edge Peg would rise up from beneath the murky depths, she would then grab their ankles and pull them under the water before dragging them to her lair and then eating them alive. Indication that Peg was beneath the water waiting for her next victim was said to come in the form of a green foam on the water's surface, known by the children as Peg Powler's Suds.

Despite the belief that Peg Powler was little more than a myth, there have been a number of sightings of a monstrous hag fitting Peg's description:

In 1754 a local man by the name of John Tallentire recorded in his diary that he had seen in the River Tees 'a creature of greenish complexion and utter horror'.

In 1767 Isaac Pennington recorded in his ship's log 'today a strange creature as sighted of the port bow. It scared all the fish away, and half my men witless.'

In 1864, Emily Jackson recorded in her diary 'I had a very strange experience today; I was attacked by a strange hag-like fish monster who came out the Tees. I believe I am beginning to go mad.'

Visitor Information

Address:
Cow Green Reservoir Car Park
Langdon Beck
County Durham
DL12 0HX

Tel: 01388 528801

Opening Hours:
Open at all reasonable times. There are free guided walks from the car park at Cow Green Reservoir daily leaving at 2 p.m. The walk takes in the dam and Cauldron Snout

How to Get There: The Cow Green Reservoir car park is situated in Upper Teesdale, 8 miles north west of Middleton-in-Teesdale, County Durham, on the B6277. Cauldron Snout Waterfall is a 2-mile walk from the car park
OS Map Reference: NY 859 296

Additional Information:
- The car park at Cow Green Reservoir contains information boards about the nature reserve, the wildlife, plant life, geology, and climate
- The 2-mile walk from the nearest car park to Cauldron Snout is rough and uneven in places, but it is a fairly gentle walk. Strong footwear and outdoor clothing are recommended
- Please keep to the path at all times when in the reserve
- There are toilets at the car park at the Cow Green Reservoir

Crook Hall

Crook Hall is a medieval manor house originally built in 1286 on land belonging to Sydgate Manor. History records that the land had previously been owned by Gilbert de Aikes, who granted it to Aimery, the son of the then Archdeacon of Durham, in 1217. In the early fourteenth century the manor became the property of Peter de Croke, which is how the Hall got its name, a corruption of which is still used to this day. The old name of Croke Hall is shown on maps of Durham as late as 1749.

By 1415 the Hall was owned by Thomas Billingham and it remained in the Billingham family until they sold it to the Mickletons in 1657. The Mickletons carried out extensive restoration work in 1671. In 1721 James Mickleton, the grandson of Christopher Mickleton who had bought the Hall into the family, died and directed in his will that Crook Hall should be sold to pay his debts.

Further improvements to Crook Hall were carried out by subsequent owners over the years, and the result is a beautiful Grade I Listed manor house which stands as a rare example of three eras of English architecture: the Medieval Hall from the original building, Jacobean improvements carried out by the Mickletons, and a Georgian house built by the Hopper family in the eighteenth century. Crook Hall's gardens attract visitors from all over the UK and have been described by Alan Titchmarsh as a 'tapestry of colourful blooms'. Despite the grandeur of the building, there is an air of mystery surrounding Crook Hall, from rumours of secret passageways lost during the centuries of rebuilding and restructuring, to one of County Durham's best known ghosts – the White Lady of Crook Hall.

The identity of the White Lady is unknown, but a previous owner of Crook Hall, Mary Hawgood, is convinced the spirit is that of the niece of Cuthbert Billingham. She is seen to glide down a disused wooden staircase in the oldest part of the Hall, the stairs coming to an abrupt stop. Her presence is also felt in the Jacobean Room.

Maggie Bell, who owns the Hall with her husband Keith, took the time to tell me of Crook Hall's ghosts:

Crook Hall's best known ghost is the White Lady; we own a letter written many years ago, although it's not dated, which tells of a grand ball in the Medieval Hall with a huge feast. As preparations for the ball were being completed and the table laid out,

Crook Hall. (By kind permission of Crook Hall)

the room was left empty for a short period of time. Suddenly there was a loud crashing coming from the room. Everything had been thrown around and broken. The letter tells that this was the work of the White Lady.

Most people know of the White Lady, but Crook Hall actually has a second ghost; the spirit of a murdered soldier who was bricked up alive in a wall in the north east corner of the Hall.

We don't believe in ghosts, but having lived at Crook Hall for sixteen or seventeen years we've experienced so many unusual happenings, too many to recall, that it does make you wonder. The most unusual experience I can think of happened five or six years ago when we used to sleep in a bedroom in the Jacobean part of the Hall. I was asleep but Keith couldn't sleep. In the early hours he became aware of a dragging sound on the Minstrel's Gallery which seemed to be coming around the corner and then stopped outside our bedroom door. Keith was convinced it was a burglar, but just as he expected the bedroom door to be burst open by the intruder he heard the sound of footsteps going upstairs – on a staircase which no longer exists!

One of Crook Hall's many gardens in autumn. (By kind permission of Crook Hall)

The Jacobean Room, Crook Hall. (By kind permission of Crook Hall)

As the footsteps reached the top of the stairs he was terrified to clearly hear the sound of footsteps on creaky floorboards in the disused attic above us. The room, which has since been restored, was at that time completely inaccessible, one of the walls had been completely removed, the window had been bricked up, and all of the floorboards had been taken up – the room had no floor.

Crook Hall has always been a place that has generated fear amongst the locals. I was told that there used to be pit behind the Hall called Cathole Pit, I'm not sure if that was its actual name, or just something that it was known by, but the children who worked down the pit lived in fear of Crook Hall. After finishing their long hours in the pit they would refuse to walk home past Crook Hall, so their mother would have to come and collect them.

The ancient wooden staircase upon which the White Lady has been seen.
(By kind permission of Crook Hall)

The Medieval Hall. (By kind permission of Crook Hall)

Visitor Information

Address:
Crook Hall & Gardens
Frankland Lane
Sidegate
Durham
DH1 5SZ

Tel: 0191 3848028
Email: info@kbacrookhall.co.uk
Website: www.crookhallgardens.co.uk

Opening Hours:
Easter weekend, 11 a.m. – 5 p.m.
May – September, open daily except Fridays and Saturdays 11 a.m. – 5 p.m.
Halloween, 31 October and 1 November 3 p.m. – dusk. Pre booking essential
Christmas, please contact the Hall or visit the website for opening dates. 1 p.m. –
dusk. Pre booking essential

How to Get There: Crook Hall is on Frankland Lane, Sidegate, a short walk from the
Gates Shopping Centre
OS Map Reference: NZ 274 433

Additional Information:
- There is pay and display parking on site
- Wheelchair access is difficult; please contact Crook Hall by telephone or email to discuss individual cases
- There is a meeting room available for bookings in the Jacobean part of the house. It will cater for twenty-six delegates. Please contact the Hall for further information
- Crook Hall is licensed for weddings which can be booked for selected Fridays and Saturdays. Guests would have exclusive access to Crook Hall from 9 a.m. – 6 p.m.
- Special events are carried out throughout the year from apple and pear picking in autumn, meeting Santa Claus at Christmas, and ghost hunts. More information is available on the website or by contacting Crook Hall
- Tickets for entry to the Hall or for the special events can be booked through the website

Darlington Civic Theatre

On Monday 2 September 1907, the New Hippodrome and Palace Theatre of Varieties was formally opened. The managing director was Signor Rino Pepi. Born in Florence, Italy, Signor Pepi had been one of Europe's greatest quick-change artistes. Queen Victoria had enjoyed his shows so much that she gave him her diamond scarf pin. Signor Pepi owned a number of theatres across the country, including three others in the North East: Bishop Auckland, Middlesbrough, and Shildon. A lot of his time was spent at the New Hippodrome along with his wife, Mary, Countess de Rossetti, and their beloved Pekinese dog.

The theatre was designed and built by Owen & Ward of Birmingham. It was constructed in local Middlesbrough red brick, and the theatre had a distinctive look due to a 64ft-high pyramid-roofed tower. This roof was designed in this way to house a huge water tank for aquatic effects which were popular at that time.

After running the theatre for a little over twenty years Signor Pepi died of lung cancer on 17 November 1927, aged only fifty-five. Signor Pepi's wife, Mary, had passed away in 1915, and the future of the New Hippodrome was uncertain.

A number of different managers came and went in the years that followed, and the growing popularity of cinema made times very hard for the theatre. The New Hippodrome struggled on until 1966, when the Borough Council of Darlington took control of the theatre, and the name was changed to Darlington Civic Theatre.

Darlington Civic Theatre celebrated its centenary in 2007, and is as popular today as it was when Signor Rino Pepi first opened the theatre's doors to the public.

It appears Signor Pepi does not want to leave the theatre as his ghost has been seen on dozens of occasions sitting in his box to the left of the stage and, in a top hat, wing collar shirt and long black coat, casts an eye on the goings on in 'his' theatre.

Signor Pepi is the best known spirit presence at the theatre, but he is far from alone as there are a number of other resident ghosts at Darlington Civic Theatre.

The spectral form of his Pekinese dog has also unusually been seen, most commonly by children, at the foot of a circular staircase. A medium during the 1980s also picked up on the spirit of the dog, explaining that the dog had been entombed within the walls of the theatre after it had passed away. In 1990, during the building of an extension which cut through the circular staircase, the skeletal remains of a small dog were discovered.

Darlington Civic Theatre. (By kind permission of Darlington Civic Theatre)

The Stage Door has been found locked inexplicably; also, the sound of jangling keys has been heard near to the door. The finger of blame has been pointed at a spirit called George, the old Stage Door keeper, who used to do his rounds on a daily basis, checking the building was securely locked.

Dressing Room 12 is in part of the theatre which was built on the remains of slum houses and sobbing has been heard in this room. A medium carried out a séance in this room in 2004 and has attributed the sobbing to a twelve-year-old girl called Arabella who lived in a building which stood on this site in the nineteenth century.

A young lady has been seen standing in the wings of the stage and watching performances. She appears as a dark shadow, but witnesses all explain that despite not being able to see any discernable features, they knew the spirit was that of a young woman. It is unknown who the lady is, but she has been seen by both staff and customers since the 1970s.

A ghost known as Jimmy by theatre staff is said to be of a man who committed suicide while working at the theatre as a Flyman (a Flyman is a technician who would raise and lower scenery using ropes). He is rarely seen, but is often 'sensed' and heard climbing up and down the ladders from the Stage to the Fly Floor.

Mark Smith was part of the Northern Ghost Investigations team that spent a night at Darlington Civic Theatre in 2008 and who witnessed some amazing phenomena:

During a cold December night, along with a handful of guests, Northern Ghost Investigations carried out an overnight investigation into Darlington Civic Theatre. A couple of strange events that occurred during the vigils of my particular group proved to be very interesting.

The first of these happened during our second vigil. Fellow NGI member Phil and myself, along with three of our guests, were sat in Signor Pepi's Box, talking in hushed tones about the ghosts that were supposed to haunt the place. At 12.34 a.m. the whole group was startled by what can only be described as the sound of a handful of gravel being forcefully thrown against the metal safety curtain that divides the stage from the auditorium.

As there was another group conducting a vigil on the stage behind the metal curtain, I presumed it must have been one of them knocking something over, so I just logged the event and planned to ask them what had happened in the break between vigils. On speaking to Carol, an NGI team member who was leading the other group, she told me that they had also been startled by the loud noise, and agreed that it sounded like a shower of small stones, but they had presumed that it was my group making the racket. Upon hearing this, Phil and I carried out a thorough investigation of the area around the safety curtain, but could find no sign of gravel or anything else that could account for the noise. There were only two groups in the area at the time and everyone was accounted for. The noise remains a mystery.

The second event that sticks in my mind occurred in Dressing Room 12. Our group was aware of the fact that this area was alleged to be the haunt of a young girl, who was believed to have lived in the slum houses that once occupied the site where this area of the theatre now stands. We sat around a small table and tried a Ouija board session in an attempt to communicate with the girl, or indeed any other spirits present. I was not surprised when the session proved fruitless. The group had started to feel a bit deflated by that point and sat around chatting about the paranormal in general.

Suddenly the temperature in the room seemed to drop, and the whole atmosphere became 'heavier'. As I looked at my fellow investigators' faces I could tell that this was felt by all present. Seizing the moment we decided to try the Ouija board once more and almost immediately the planchette responded by moving swiftly to 'yes' when asked directly if there was a spirit present that wanted to communicate.

One of the guests and I distinctly felt a cold draft blow across our hands whilst touching the planchette. We asked if the spirit present was that of the little girl and the planchette responded by again pointing to 'yes'. When asked her age, the planchette pointed to '8'. When she was asked to spell out her name the planchette pointed to 'H' and then 'U'. Further questioning revealed that the 'girl' seemed to be a happy little soul who enjoyed coming to watch the other 'living' children who use the dressing room.

The session was then interrupted by one of the guests jumping up claiming that she had been prodded quite hard in the spine, through the open back of the chair on which she was sitting. The atmosphere then gradually returned to how it had been at the start of the vigil and there was no more response from the board.

It is interesting to note that other than the fact she was a young girl, this information does not match the stories of the girl that is supposed to be present in the dressing room; her name is alleged to be Arabella and she is aged twelve, not eight.

Up until that point I have never had any 'success' with a Ouija board, other than seeing perfectly normal, small subconscious movements or witnessing blatant 'glass pushing' from participants (either purposefully or not). I am as certain as I can be that none of the group were moving the planchette and I studied their fingertips closely. We had taken turns at removing each of our fingers from the planchette as it was moving and it continued to move. There was also a point when none of the guests had their fingers on the planchette (just myself and fellow NGI member Phil, who is as sceptical of such things as I am), and it still continued to move with speed. All in all, a very interesting experience.

Visitor Information

Address:
Darlington Civic Theatre
Parkgate
Darlington
DL1 1RR

Tel: 01325 486555
Website: www.darlington.gov.uk/Culture/arts/

How to Get There: From Parkgate, go past the entrance to Darlington railway station on your left and the Civic Theatre is located approximately 300 yards on your right
OS Map Reference: NZ 292 144

Additional Information:
- Signor Pepi's Bar and Conservatory Bar are open one hour before performances for pre-show drinks. For your convenience the theatre offers a pre-order system for interval drinks from both bars
- Before the performance and during the interval there is also a wide variety of ice cream and confectionery available from the kiosks
- There is no food available
- If you are a wheelchair user please make the theatre aware when booking
- Guide dogs are welcome and a bowl of water can be provided
- Some performances are sign language interpreted or audio-described, please check with the Box Office
- What's On brochures are available in large print, audio and Braille
- There is an infra-red system in the auditorium at the Civic Theatre which requires a special receiver, available free from the Front of House staff. Please remember to ask at the time of booking
- For people with hearing aids there is an audio loop in the theatre. If you are attending a performance because it is sign language interpreted please let the Box Office staff know when booking so that they can give you seats in the best place
- Tours of the theatre can be arranged, as well as ghost tours. Please contact the theatre for further information

Darlington Railway Centre & c. Museum

*N*orth Road Station opened in 1842 to serve the Stockton & Darlington Railway, the world's first steam-powered passenger railway. The station was in use for over a century until the railway network was reduced in the 1960s, and the station closed in 1962. The building was left abandoned, and as the years passed, the fabric of the building began to rot and vandals smashed every window. So bad was the damage that it looked as though North Road station might have to be demolished. However, in the early 1970s local railway enthusiasts rallied support from like-minded groups across the country and successfully saved the station. It opened as a railway museum devoted to the area formerly served by the North Eastern Railway, with particular reference to the Stockton & Darlington Railway. Exhibits include George Stephenson's 'Locomotion No. 1', one of the oldest surviving steam engines in the world, and the first ever steam-powered passenger locomotive.

To the ghost hunter the most interesting piece of history within the museum is the story of the building's resident ghost, a chilling tale which has survived for over 150 years. On a bitterly cold December night in the 1850s, the station's night watchman, James Durham, was doing his rounds within the North Road station. Durham saw a man leave a coalhouse and head towards the Porter's Cellar. He was dressed in a station clerk's uniform with a black retriever following close behind. There should have been no other station staff on site so Durham approached the man, demanding to know what he was doing there. As he neared, the 'intruder' turned to Durham and punched him hard in the face. Durham felt blood flow from his nose, and tried to return a blow to his assailant. His fist went straight through the man and struck a wall; Durham recoiled in both pain and terror. As he checked his scuffed knuckles, the phantom station clerk ordered his dog to attack and the obedient retriever sank his teeth deep into Durham's leg. Durham cried out in pain, and then the ghost and his dog simply turned around and walked through a wall. Durham looked down to see how bad the dog bite was, but there was no mark and the pain had stopped. He felt his nose, but there was no blood.

George Stephenson's Locomotion No. 1. (By kind permission of Darlington Railway Museum)

The Entrance to the Porter's Cellar. (By kind permission of Darlington Railway Museum)

He told his story to colleagues, who were initially convinced that he had either imagined the whole thing, or that he was simply making it up. However, when he described the man and the dog to them, they quickly realised that this was not the case; he had perfectly described a man by the name of Thomas Munro Winter, who had committed suicide at the station in early 1845. His lifeless body was found in a water closet along with the pistol he had used to shoot himself, and his corpse was moved to the Porter's Cellar until it could be transferred to the morgue.

Durham, a teetotaller, relayed his experience to the Society of Psychic Research a number of years later, and they went on record in 1891 as describing it as 'the most thrilling encounter that has come to our notice'.

Sightings of a shadowy figure, with his faithful black hound following closely behind, continue to this day.

Visitor Information

Address:
Darlington Railway Centre & Museum
North Road Station
Darlington
DL3 6ST

Tel: 01325 460532
Email: museum@darlington.gov.uk
Website: www.head-of-steam.co.uk

Opening Hours:
April – September, Monday. Closed, Tuesday – Sunday 10 a.m. – 4 p.m.
October – March, Monday – Thursday. Closed, Friday – Sunday 11 a.m. – 3 p.m.

How to Get There: The museum is 1 mile from Darlington town centre on the A167 and is well signposted
OS Map Reference: NZ 289 157

Additional Information:
- Free onsite parking
- Railway café, open Monday – Sunday 11a.m. – 3 p.m.
- Wheelchair access to most parts of the museum
- Baby changing facilities within the museum main building
- Gift shop selling a wide range of souvenirs and memorabilia

Durham Castle

*D*urham Castle, along with the breathtaking cathedral, are very much icons of the city, and county, of Durham. The present castle was built in 1072 as one of the first fortified castles commissioned by William the Conqueror during his 'Harrying of the North'. The building work was overseen by Waltheof, the Earl of Northumberland, and a motte and bailey castle was built with the purpose of defending the peninsular formed by the meander in the River Wear.

The previous year, William Walcher had been appointed Bishop of Durham and the castle was to be his seat, as the office of Bishop of Durham was appointed by the King to exercise royal authority on his behalf. When Waltheof was executed in 1075, for his part in the 'Revolt of the Earls' against William, Walcher was also appointed earl, becoming the first Prince Bishop. Bishop Walcher had a Hall built upon the site of the current Great Hall. He also built the Undercroft and the Norman Chapel. Walcher was a good man, but proved to be an incapable leader; this contributed to his murder in Gateshead in 1081.

The lands ruled by the bishops became known as the County Palatine of Durham, a defensive zone between England and the Northumbria-Scottish border. Due to its remoteness from London, the County Palatine was ruled over by the Prince Bishop, who possessed the powers of a king, including having the authority to hold their own parliaments, raise their own armies, administer their own laws, and mint their own coins.

In the year 1300 Prince Bishop Antony Bek said, 'There are two kings in England, namely the Lord King of England, wearing a crown in sign of his regality and the Lord Bishop of Durham wearing a mitre in place of a crown, in sign of his regality in the diocese of Durham'. Bek built the present Great Hall in 1284, which was then extended by Bishop Thomas Hatfield in 1350, making it the largest Great Hall in Britain – until it was shortened at the end of the fifteenth century by Bishop Richard Foxe. However, it is still 14 metres high and over 30 metres long.

In the Tudor period, Bishop Cuthbert Tunstall added the chapel in 1540 and the Galleries which bear his name. Durham Castle suffered considerable dilapidation during the Civil War, and when England became a Commonwealth in 1649, Durham Castle was seized by Oliver Cromwell and sold to the Lord Mayor of London.

Durham Castle at night, overlooking the River Wear.
(By kind permission of Durham University)

With the English Restoration in 1660, the castle was handed back to the Bishops of Durham. Improvements were carried out by the then Bishop John Cosin, who constructed the Black Staircase, and his successor Bishop Nathaniel Crewe.

When the University of Durham was founded in 1837, the Bishop of Durham, William Van Mildert, gave Durham Castle to the university. The Keep, then a ruin, was rebuilt in 1840 by the architect Anthony Salvin to the same floor plan as the original Norman keep, to provide student accommodation.

In the late 1920s it was discovered that the north west corner of the castle was in imminent danger of sliding into the River Wear and urgent action was taken to install new foundations. The castle remains in the care of Durham University to this day.

One of the most memorable moments of a visit to Durham Castle is your first glimpse of the magnificent Black Staircase. It is named for the dark oak of which it was made, and is 57ft high. It is one of the most impressive staircases of its time in England. What's more, it appears that the Black Staircase may have a dark secret; the ghostly figure of a woman has been witnessed gliding up the staircase on countless occasions since the seventeenth century. Local legend tells that this is the spirit of

Durham Castle Keep. (By kind permission of Durham University)

Isabella, the wife of William Van Mildert. She fell down the staircase, breaking her neck. She is also seen in the Norman Gallery, but is only seen from the knees up due to the difference in floor levels as a result of the rebuilding in 1840.

A less well-known ghost story is that of Frederick Copeman. David Butler runs the Durham Ghost Walk and told me of the tragic circumstances which led to Frederick haunting Durham Castle forever more:

Frederick John Copeman was one of the first students at the new University of Durham in the early nineteenth century, when the castle became University College, and he lived in the highest room at the top of the Black Staircase, called by other students the 'Crow's Nest'. As the time for his final exams came closer he became increasingly worried. He took the exams and waited with trepidation for the results. Then, as today, degree results were pinned-up on the notice-board outside the University Library on Palace Green and he hurried to look at them.

The results lists for each subject show those with first class degrees at the top, and the other classes of degree in order below, and if a name does not appear on the list then it means a total failure.

The entrance to the courtyard of Durham Castle. (By kind permission of Durham University)

*Since the death of Frederick Copeman the results lists are
pinned up very carefully to avoid pages overlapping.
(By kind permission of Durham University)*

Frederick could not find his name on the list and went back to his room in deep despair. After a period of agitated thought he rushed from the room and down the Black Staicase. Ignoring everyone around him, he ran across Palace Green to the cathedral, climbed the steps to the top of the tower and threw himself off.

The ghost of Frederick Copeman is unusual in that it is not visible, but his ghostly footsteps can be heard pacing backwards and forwards across the floor of the room at the top of the Black Staircase re-living his last few tormented moments alive, then, with a crash, the door is thrown open, and the footsteps are heard running down the wooden stairs.

Since Frederick Copeman's death, and to this day, the cathedral tower is kept locked when degree results are posted up. The Crow's Nest room is now never used as a student room, but only used as a stationery store. But the ironic twist in the story is that when the results lists were examined later, it was discovered that the sheet pinned above his had accidentally covered up Frederick Copeman's name at the top of the list – he had actually gained a first-class degree.

Visitor Information

Address:
University College
Durham Castle
Palace Green
Durham
DH1 3RW

Tel: 0191 3343800
Website: www.dur.ac.uk/university.college/

Opening Hours:
The castle is only accessible on the tours that are run at regular intervals. The tour times are as follows:

Tours during University Terms
Tours are normally available every afternoon of the week at 2 p.m., 3 p.m. and 4 p.m. For full details of term dates go to www.dur.ac.uk/dates.

Tours during University vacations
Tours are normally available every morning of the week at 10 a.m., 11 a.m. and 12 noon, and in the afternoons, when there are no commercial activities, from 2 p.m. – 5 p.m.

How to Get There: The castle is in Durham city centre and is well signposted
OS Map Reference: NZ 272 423

Additional Information:
- Due to the nature and layout of the castle, the interior is completely inaccessible to wheelchairs
- There is a 360 degree virtual tour of the castle on the website
- Durham Castle caters for wedding receptions, banquets, dinner dances, and other special events. For more information please contact Event Durham on 0800 289970 or email event@durham.ac.uk
- During student vacations it is possible to book bed and breakfast accommodation in Durham Castle. A wide range of different rooms are available, from standard rooms with shared facilities, to magnificent state rooms, which are available throughout the year. More information can be found on the University website
- There is no parking at Durham Castle; parking can be found on Palace Green just outside the castle entrance at a daily charge. There are also a number of public car parks nearby
- The Durham Ghost Walk takes place every Monday evening at 7.30 p.m. during the summer, starting at the Durham Tourist Information Centre in Millennium Place. There are also Halloween and Christmas Ghost Walks. For further details contact David Butler on 0191 3861500

Egglestone Abbey

Egglestone Abbey is a twelfth-century abbey standing on the borders of Yorkshire and County Durham. The ruined remains are those of the abbey church and its adjoining cloister. The abbey was founded in 1195 by the Premonstratensians, who wore white habits and were commonly referred to as the White Canons.

Around 100 years after the founding of Egglestone Abbey the church was expanded and rebuilt, which was common with many monasteries of the time, and it's this later church that stands today. The centre of the church, known as the crossing, has virtually disappeared, apart from one wall of the south transept dating from around 1275. The standing walls are all of a good height and the foundations of the walls which have long since vanished are still visible, allowing visitors to visualise the size and magnificence of the working abbey. The central area of the church has a number of grave slabs of canons long deceased, the names and inscriptions of which are mostly illegible due to age and the harsh weather that the abbey regularly suffers because of the exposed position it holds. There is also an elaborately sculptured tomb chest, which was for Sir Ralph Bowes of Streatlam who died in 1512.

Egglestone Abbey was always a poor abbey and struggled to maintain the required twelve canons. The financial hardship was worsened by raids by Scottish invaders, and disputes throughout the Middle Ages; many costly repairs were required during this period of the abbey's history.

In 1536 Henry VIII began to close down all Roman Catholic Abbeys, monasteries and convents across England in a bid to reduce the Church's power; this was known as the Dissolution of the Monasteries. In 1540 Egglestone Abbey was dissolved, and in 1548 the lands were granted by the king to Robert Strelley and his wife Fredeswide. Strelley set about converting some of the buildings into a grand private house, and he demolished the church tower because he felt it spoilt the view from his new home. Robert Strelley died in January 1554 and the site proceeded to pass through many different hands over the years that followed, and the building has suffered due to so many alterations. It was occupied until 1770 when the Morritt family, who had purchased Rokeby Park the previous year, bought the abbey and made use of the remains as an ornamental focal point of their estate. During the

Egglestone Abbey. (By kind permission of English Heritage)

nineteenth century much of the abbey was pulled down and the stone reused elsewhere, including paving the stable yard at Rokeby Hall. Stonework was still being reclaimed from Egglestone Abbey as recently as 1905. The site is now a Scheduled Ancient Monument and is maintained by English Heritage.

In the 1300s, a novice monk named Brother Martin lived at Egglestone Abbey. The monks were allowed to leave the abbey to go for walks or go fishing in the nearby river. One moonlit evening the monk decided to go for a walk along the riverside. He met a young girl who tried to talk to him but he turned and fled from the young lady, so as to not break his vows.

For a short while Martin never ventured from the abbey, but he couldn't get the young girl's smile and piercing eyes out of his mind. Eventually, the temptation proved too much for him and he went for a stroll along the Tees, the same time and same route as he had previously taken, in the hope of seeing her again. Sure enough, he met the girl again but this time he did talk; he apologised for his previous behaviour and they talked and laughed for hours until it had became dark. They promised to meet again the next evening.

They met the next evening, and the evening after that, and the one after that, and eventually they became lovers. They met every night at their secret place under the trees next to the river. Martin began to feel guilty whenever he wasn't with her. Another monk was getting worried by Martin's unusual behaviour and his pale complexion. He decided to go and see Martin one night and, as he approached Martin's cell, he heard weeping. He entered the cell and asked Martin what was wrong. Martin confessed his misdeeds and was advised to stop these meetings at once; from that moment on he shouldn't leave the abbey grounds and should put the girl from his mind.

For several weeks Martin remained in his cell, sobbing and praying for forgiveness for his sins. One stormy evening it all became too much for the monk, he ran from his cell out towards the secret place in the hope of seeing the girl. Sure enough she was there waiting for him, as she had done every night ever since their last meeting. She was overcome with joy when she saw him approaching, but he was sweating, pale and breathless. She asked if he was feeling himself, if he had been ill. She asked why he looked at her in such an intense manner. He suddenly lost it; he grabbed her and shouted at her, accusing her of being evil, sent from the devil to tempt him. He lashed out at her, screaming in rage. She tried to run, terrified that the man she loved had gone mad. He caught her and wrestled her to the ground; she was screaming for help but no one was around. He told her to be quiet, her screams continued, his hands found her throat and soon enough she was silent. He had killed her.

The Tees were in full flow as the rain came down and the wind roared. Sobbing, Martin dragged her lifeless body to the water's edge and threw her in. For a minute or two she floated on the water's surface and then the rush of the water took her body under and away forever.

Wet, shaking and mumbling hysterically, the monk staggered back up to the abbey. His absence from prayer the following morning didn't go unnoticed and the monks found Martin in his cell, delirious with fever and gravely ill. His habit was torn, soaked through and covered in leaves and grass. The monks couldn't understand how he was in this condition. With their care Martin recovered within a week, but he would not talk. No matter how often the monks tried to converse with Martin he would not utter one word.

Then one evening there was a great storm – lightning illuminating the sky, and thunder crashing loudly above the abbey. Martin clambered out of his bed, and in a trace-like state he left the abbey towards the Tees for one last time. He headed to their secret place. As the rain lashed down and the sky lit up with the constant flash of lightning, he prayed to God for forgiveness then he snapped. He ran down the steep slope and threw himself, with a great scream, into the merciless waters below.

This may seem like a story passed down from generation to generation of locals in the area, but this doesn't explain the regular sighting of a ghostly monk seen moving around the ruins or sometimes rushing down from the abbey to the Tees just as dusk approaches. When the river is in flood a monk and a ghostly young lady are often seen drifting above the water. Much more often, however, you can hear screams of agony coming from the steep banks of the Tees.

The Novices Room. (By kind permission of English Heritage)

Jonathan Horner of Yarm told me of the night he spent at Egglestone Abbey with a friend in August 2009, in the hope of experiencing something supernatural:

> I myself visited Egglestone Abbey whilst on a camping trip. Some locals had told a friend and I that the abbey was haunted so we decided to pay a visit to the abbey late one night to investigate.
>
> We were stood in the ruins at around midnight in the only part of the abbey with a roof, the Novices Room. Whilst there, my friend was staring at something and appeared to be transfixed. I spoke to him but he didn't answer, I touched his shoulder and he jumped. He seemed shaken and explained that he had seen what looked like a young man and lady sat perched on part of the ruin just outside of the Novices Room; they didn't move in the time he watched them but they just seemed to fade away before his eyes. Shortly after this he wanted to leave.
>
> When I got back from our camping trip, I did some research into Egglestone Abbey's ghosts. I found the story of Brother Martin who had a secret love affair with a girl, and still haunts the grounds and the Tees. My friend saw what he believed to be a young man and a young lady; Brother Martin and his lover reunited in death perhaps?

Visitor Information

Address:
Egglestone Abbey
Barnard Castle
County Durham
DL12 9TN

Tel: 0191 2691200
Website: www.english-heritage.org.uk

Opening Hours:
All year 10 a.m. – 6 p.m., closed 24 – 26 December and 1 January

How to Get There: Egglestone Abbey is 1 mile south of Barnard Castle, on a minor road just off the B6277
OS Map Reference: NZ 063 150

Additional Information:
- Egglestone Abbey is suitable for visitors in wheelchairs
- Dogs are allowed on leads
- There is a picnic area
- There is free parking
- There is no shop, nor are there any toilets

Finchale Priory

*T*he first building on the site of Finchale Priory was a hermitage created by Godric, dedicated to John the Baptist in the early twelfth century. He chose a scenic spot on the banks of the River Wear which was to become his home for almost sixty years. He had not always been a man of God; he was born in Walpole in Norfolk and grew up to become a pedlar and then a sailor. After many years at sea Godric visited Lindisfarne; this visit changed his life forever and he dedicated the remainder of his life to Christianity. He went on a number of pilgrimages around the Mediterranean and to Jerusalem before returning to England where he sought permission from Ranulf Flambard, the Bishop of Durham, to allow him to build a hermitage at Finchale.

Godric lived a simple, lonely existence, choosing to live and sleep outside regardless of the weather. In 1160 Godric became very ill and was confined to his bed where he was cared for by the monks of Durham until his death a decade later on 21 May 1170, at the age of 105. He was initially interred in Durham, but his remains were later moved to the stone chapel of St John the Baptist at Finchale, built towards the end of Godric's life. In death Godric became a popular medieval saint, although he was never formally canonised. He was best remembered for his kindness to animals; he would do anything to help and protect the fauna that lived near his simple home. One tale recalls a time when he hid a stag from hunters that had chased it through the forest.

In 1196 Godric's simple hermitage at Finchale became a Benedictine priory, dependent on Durham Cathedral. Two monks of Durham moved to Finchale, where they found a small church, a dam, and a mill. Work began in the latter half of the thirteenth century to build a bigger church and the site remained under construction for over 300 years.

Finchale had no more than four monks in residence at any one time, although it was not uncommon for monks to travel from Durham Cathedral to stay at Finchale. Finchale remained a priory until 1535, which saw the dissolution of the lesser monasteries.

Fragments of the church today date back to the twelfth century, built towards the end of Godric's life, with other remains dating from the mid-fourteenth century. Some of the temporary buildings constructed in the late twelfth century for the first prior of Finchale remain. There are some well-preserved heavily decorated capitals on the arcade columns, and beautiful tracery in the filled-in nave arches of the church.

Finchale Priory. (By kind permission of English Heritage)

Timeslips have been reported to occur when crossing this bridge.
(By kind permission of English Heritage)

Finchale Priory is one of the few places in the world where time slips have been reported on a number of occasions; a very rare, extremely frightening, paranormal occurrence where witnesses are taken back in time and given a glimpse of their current location in a bygone age. This is said to occur on the bridge next to Finchale Priory that crosses the River Wear and individuals have claimed to have seen Finchale Priory, no longer ruined, but how it would have appeared when it was in use as a priory, with monks wandering between the buildings. Witnesses have described sensations such as sounds seeming muffled, colours appearing muted, and a feeling of depression.

There is also a legend of a club-footed ghost called Slewfoot who has been seen throughout the ruined priory.

Visitor Information

Address:
Finchale Priory
Framwellgate Moor
Durham
DH1 5SH

Tel: 0191 3863828
Website: www.english-heritage.org.uk

Opening Hours:
1 April – 30 September Saturday, Sunday, and Bank Holidays 10 a.m. – 5 p.m.

How to Get There: 3 miles north east of Durham on a minor road off the A167
OS Map Reference: NZ 296 471

Additional Information:
- There are toilets in Finchale Farmhouse (not managed by English Heritage)
- There is a gift shop
- Guide dogs permitted
- Parking areas for disabled visitors. Parking is 75m from the priory, but disabled visitors may be set down at site entrance
- Educational visits can be arranged; please contact the priory for further information
- There is a tearoom in Finchale Farmhouse (not managed by English Heritage) and a picnic area within the priory grounds

Jimmy Allen's

Jimmy Allen's is a popular nightclub in the heart of Durham City along the River Wear. It is built into the remains of an old prison beneath Elvet Bridge, and it is from the prison's most famous inmate that the nightclub takes its name.

Jimmy Allen was born in 1733, and was an adopted member of the Faas, a famous clan of gypsies who lived in the Cheviot Hills. Jimmy was taught the Northumbrian pipes by his adopted family and he was a natural, quickly becoming a very talented player. He became the official piper to the Duchess of Northumberland, a position he held for two years.

Jimmy, however, had his vices; he drank too much, he gambled, and he had an eye for the ladies. Jimmy began to steal from the women he romanced, and then he progressed to cattle rustling. Jimmy enlisted in the British Army, only to desert shortly afterwards. He was caught and imprisoned. Jimmy escaped and ran off to Edinburgh, where he was tracked down, and locked up again. He successfully escaped for a second time, this time making his way to Dublin, from where it is believed he made his way abroad, as far as India, making a living from his extraordinary skills as a piper.

In 1803 Jimmy was arrested for a third and final time at Jedburgh for stealing a horse in Gateshead. He was taken to Durham and was tried and sentenced to death, but for reasons unknown this was reduced to life imprisonment. He spent seven years in a cell at the House of Correction beneath Elvet Bridge with only rats and his pipes for company. In 1810 Jimmy was found dead, aged seventy-seven. Ironically, a pardon had been issued by the Prince Regent, arriving three days after he had passed away. Jimmy's ghost is believed to remain in the cell to this day, and if you listen carefully you can still hear his pipes.

The cells at the House of Correction were mainly used to hold men and women condemned to death, who were then taken to the local market square and hanged. It appears that Jimmy is not the only tormented soul to remain in the nightclub which bears his name; shadowy figures have been seen on a regular basis throughout the building, and people have reported hearing a female voice whispering in their ear.

Jimmy Allen's. (By kind permission of Jimmy Allen's)

Jimmy Allen's was built into the remains of a prison, and evidence of this can still be seen.
(Photograph by Lee Foster, by kind permission of Jimmy Allen's)

Visitor Information

Address:
Jimmy Allen's
19-21 Elvet Bridge
Durham
DH1 3AA

Tel: 0191 3757574

Opening Hours:
8 p.m. – late daily

How to Get There: Jimmy Allen's is in the centre of Durham City beneath Elvet
Bridge, on the Saddler Street side
OS Map Reference: NZ 274 424

Additional Information
- Entry to Jimmy Allen's is free

The King's Hotel

Originally a coaching inn opened in 1611, the King's Hotel, in the centre of Darlington, is proud to have two resident ghosts: Mary and Albert.

Albert began working at the hotel in 1823 as the hotel's butler. He took great pride in his work and he was well liked by the lords and ladies of the day, so much so that one gentleman who frequently stayed at the hotel presented Albert with one of his cats as a gift.

A clumsy young chambermaid named Mary joined the service at the hotel and Albert became infuriated with her dropping trays of glasses and constantly running late. However, her radiant smile and gentle teasing soon won Albert over and they fell in love. Albert and Mary could often be seen walking through Darlington arm-in-arm and there was talk of a Christmas engagement. However, in the autumn Mary inexplicably vanished. Albert was heartbroken; he could not understand why she had gone and wondered if it was something he had done wrong. His friends tried to reassure him that Mary would return to him soon, but he would never see Mary again as he went to his room, got into bed and died.

In the weeks after Albert's passing many of the guests reported a sensation of being 'tucked in' by unseen hands. One regular guest was convinced that it was Albert continuing to serve the hotel in death as he had in life.

The original hotel was pulled down in 1890; it was rebuilt and re-opened in 1893. By now it was accepted that Albert's spirit remained at the hotel, with a number of staff identifying the ghostly butler on the fourth floor of the building. But the rebuilding seemed to have disturbed something else otherworldly as staff and guests became aware of a second phantom on the third floor of the hotel. People had reported a sound like glasses being broken, followed by a female sobbing. Some had even seen a ghostly young lady running away from the noise, but it was only when a long-serving housekeeper saw this for herself that she immediately identified the ghostly young lady as Albert's lost love – Mary. To this day it's never been established what happened to Mary on that autumn day when she simply vanished, never to be seen alive again; it's been suggested that she may have been murdered, or that she had a secret that she couldn't bring herself to share with Albert so she ran away.

Albert and Mary continue to walk the corridors at the King's Hotel to this very day, and up until recent years visitors have still reported a feeling of being tucked in by Albert.

The King's Hotel prior to the devastating fire of August 2008.
(Photograph provided courtesy of the King's Hotel)

Disaster struck the King's Hotel at 12.30 a.m. on 15 August 2008 as a huge fire broke out. At first guests tried to ignore the fire alarms, assuming it to be a false alarm as the previous night the alarms had inexplicably gone off twice. However, this was no false alarm, and as one of the worst fires in Darlington's history began to consume the King's Hotel, the sixty-three people within the hotel were quickly evacuated.

By 2 a.m., the fire was at its height. A huge plume of acrid smoke rising hundreds of feet into the air hung over the town centre, lit from below by the orange glow of the flames. The fire could be clearly seen from Scotch Corner, 11 miles away.

At 5 p.m. the following day, the fire – seventeen hours after it had begun – was finally put out. The King's Hotel had been badly ravaged by the fire with the fourth floor and the roof being destroyed completely.

A joint investigation was carried out by Durham Police and the County Durham & Darlington Fire and Rescue Service, and it was established that the fire began on the fourth floor, but the definite cause of the blaze could not be determined.

I spent an afternoon at the King's Hotel in the company of hotel supervisor Mike Noble and he told me that staff are in no doubt as to the cause of the fire – Albert. Some members of staff believe that Albert may have not approved of refurbishments in recent years to the building that he has occupied for almost 200 years, with some having since felt themselves being pushed while on the fourth floor. Less than a month prior to the fire, the hotel changed its name from the King's Head Hotel, which it had previously been known as for over 100 years. This may have been one change too many for Albert.

Mike assured me that despite the loss of the fourth floor Albert still remains at the King's Hotel, and members of the night staff have seen him throughout the remaining areas of the hotel.

Work is underway to repair the areas of the hotel destroyed in the fire, and the hotel is open for bookings as usual in the interim period.

Visitor Information

Address:
The King's Hotel
Priestgate
Darlington
County Durham
DL1 1NW

Tel: 01325 380222
Email: reservations@kingsdarlington.com
Website: www.kingsheaddarlington.com

How to Get There: The King's Hotel is found on Priestgate in the town centre of Darlington
OS Map Reference: NZ 289 145

Additional Information
- The King's Hotel has twenty-six *en-suite* bedrooms. All bedrooms have a direct dial telephone, tea and coffee-making facilities, trouser press, iron and ironing board, and hair dryer
- Pets are not allowed (only guide dogs)
- Award-winning secure free covered car parking facilities
- Complimentary high-speed internet access
- A virtual tour of the King's Head is accessible on the hotel's website

Kirkcarrion

High up on the Lunedale ridge, dominating the skyline for miles around, stands the Scots pine-covered tumulus of Kirkcarrion, one of Teesdale's major Bronze Age burial sites. In 1804 the mound was excavated and a small chamber was discovered containing an urn. The urn was found to contain charred bones and some unidentifiable dark matter. Mr C. Raine of Lonton, Lord Strathmore's bailiff, marked the location of the burial by planting the pine trees, and the urn was sent to Streatlam Castle. The burial mound is believed to have been created in around 1400 BC, and the remains are thought to be those of a Brigantian Chieftain named Caryn. The Brigantes were independent, self-governing tribes who had settled in the north of England during the Bronze Age.

Caryn is thought to have been killed in battle and his body burned atop a funeral pyre. His ashes and burnt bones were placed inside the urn and his tribe will have worked night and day to pack stones and earth over the urn, creating a huge mound or tumulus.

It has been said that no matter how wild the wind, there is an area within the circle of ancient trees where no wind ever blows. Kirkcarrion is also believed to be haunted by the restless spirit of Caryn, lamenting the disturbance of his prehistoric resting place.

Kirkcarrion.

Visitor Information

How to Get There: Kirkcarrion is 1 mile south west of Middleton in Teesdale. Take the B6276 to Lunedale. Once parked, follow the public footpaths to Kirkcarrion
OS Map Reference: NY 939 237

Additional Information:
- Middleton-in-Teesdale is 1 mile away from Kirkcarrion and has two hotels, a number of guest houses, tearooms, and shops
- Middleton-in-Teesdale also has a tourist information centre. Kirkcarrion is very popular with walkers and the tourist information centre has a variety of books and maps containing information on Kirkcarrion, and the best route to the summit

Lumley Castle

*L*umley Castle was the creation of the man from whom it took its name – Sir Ralph Lumley. Sir Ralph was well known throughout the north; a brave soldier, he was knighted in 1385, and, in 1388, helped to defend Berwick-upon-Tweed from the Scots. Later that year he led the attack at the Battle of Otterburn and, despite fighting courageously, was captured and imprisoned in Scotland.

He was released the following year and returned home to the manor house his ancestors had built. Due to the uncertain times, he sought permission from the Bishop of Durham to turn his manor house into a castle. This was approved and work began immediately. Nine years later, in 1398, Sir Ralph's castle was completed.

In January 1400 Sir Ralph and his son, Thomas, partook in a conspiracy to kill King Henry IV and replace him with Richard II. The plan was to attack the new king during a tournament at Windsor Castle. However, Edward, Earl of Rutland, betrayed the plot, and the king and his family escaped to London and the rebels were arrested. Sir Ralph and his son were stripped of their titles and beheaded.

The lands belonging to Sir Ralph were forfeited to the Earl of Somerset until his death in 1421. The earl had no son to inherit his estates, so Lumley Castle and its land reverted to the Lumley family, and specifically Sir Ralph's grandson, Thomas.

The castle is still owned by the Lumley family, but in 1976 tennancy was granted to 'No Ordinary Hotels' and it was turned into the fifty-nine bedroom five-star hotel it is today. The castle is full of dark corridors and has a medieval atmosphere enhanced by the rooms being made up in a period style, and the staff wearing period costume.

Lumley Castle is famous the world over for its resident ghost – Lily of Lumley, Sir Ralph's wife. The couple were Lollards, followers of John Wycliffe's preaching of a New Testament Gospel. When Sir Ralph was away in Berwick-upon-Tweed two priests visited Lady Lumley and tried to bring her back to the Catholic fold. She was strong willed and politely thanked the priests for their visit and explained she had no intent of returning to Catholicism. The priests were concerned for her soul, so lured her into a bedroom, where they murdered her, carried her body to the basement and threw her down the well.

The priests found a very ill local young woman and took her to a convent near Finchale Priory, saying that she was indeed Lady Lumley. The woman died shortly afterwards and when Sir Ralph returned from Berwick he was informed by the two priests that his wife had left to become a nun and died soon after.

This is where the truth behind the legend has became muddied over the centuries; some incarnations of the story tell that Sir Ralph believed the priests and they got away with the murder of his wife. However, other versions of the legend claim that Sir Ralph was furious with the priests for taking his wife away from Lumley Castle and had them executed. It's possible that the latter is what actually occurred as this would account for the sightings of ghostly monks walking in single file throughout the castle grounds.

The well where Lily of Lumley's body still remains to this day is now covered by a pane of glass, but guests can still look down it. It is said that every night her ghost comes up the well and walks throughout the castle. Her footsteps are heard on landings and even in rooms.

Lumley Castle made news headlines worldwide in June 2005 when the Australian cricket team spent a terrifying night at the hotel. All-rounder Shane Watson was so scared that he slept on the floor of his team-mate's room. Australian media officer Belinda Denenett admitted to journalists that several of the players were uneasy in the hotel. She went on to tell reporters that she actually saw ghosts for herself:

> I was woken at 4 a.m. by my phone, and noticed the blind at the window had opened. I looked out of the window and saw a procession of white people walking past. It was amazing, very scary. I pulled the blind back down and returned to bed, the blind suddenly opened and when I looked over there was someone looking in through the window.

This was not the first instance of a cricket team being frightened by the hotel's resident spirits; in 2000 three of the West Indies touring team that were staying at the hotel, including captain Jimmy Adams, were so scared they checked out in the middle of the night.

Haunting Breaks have organised a number of paranormal investigations at Lumley Castle, and I spoke to the company's director, Carol Bowen, about what occurred during a memorable investigation in January 2006:

> Amazingly, a full spectral apparition of a little girl was seen. She was walking along the corridor and heading towards the staircase; she appeared to be about five or six years old and dressed in nineteenth-century costume.
>
> In Room 63 one guest reported hearing noises. They took a photograph, and the following morning found the picture was covered with orbs, so much so, that it appeared as though it was snowing in the room.
>
> During dinner a couple of guests commented on headaches and strange feelings. Two of them had to retire to the bar area and fairly quickly started to feel better. Photographs were taken during this phenomena and a certain amount of orbs were captured.

Lumley Castle. (By kind permission of Lumley Castle)

Later in the dining room we conducted a vigil and we experienced strange movement and lights. One of the guests, who had previously been a complete sceptic, was astounded to experience what he believed to be a voice whisper in his ear. We asked for a noise to confirm communication and another guest said she saw a shadow move towards a particular chair. We immediately took photographs of the chair and an orb was captured in the middle of the seat.

The surrounding area is also a haven for paranormal activity; there is a tale of a headless horseman that rides from Lumley Castle to Finchale Priory. The identity of this headless phantom is unknown, but he has been reported a number of times, most commonly on stormy nights.

This glass panel covers the well in which Lily of Lumley's body was disposed.
(By kind permission of Lumley Castle)

One of the many dark corridors which add to the medieval atmosphere within Lumley Castle.
(By kind permission of Lumley Castle)

Sounds of a battle have been heard in the castle grounds and nearby woodland, the sound of sword clashing with sword, horses charging, and the cries of dying men.

One of the best known ghost stories in County Durham occurred at Lumley Mill, which has long since been destroyed, and tells of the murder of Anne Walker. The year was 1630 and John Grahame was working hard one night at the mill when suddenly he noticed a chill in the air and felt he was no longer alone. He turned and came face to face with a young woman in her late teens or early twenties; her long dress was soaked in blood and she was bleeding badly from five large head-wounds. John had a horrific realisation that there was no way anyone could survive such injuries and, resisting the urge to flee, he plucked up the courage to ask what she wanted of him.

She told him that she had been betrayed by his neighbour, her uncle, John Walker. She said she had been asked by Walker to go to with a collier called Mark Sharpe who would look after her. However, he had taken her out to moorland and when her back was turned he had killed her with a pickaxe. He concealed the murder weapon under a bank and threw her body down a mine; he struggled to get her blood from her clothes so hid those also. The ghost begged the miller to tell the authorities of the crime and said that if he didn't then she would haunt him forever.

John Grahame ran home as fast as he could, but he could not sleep; his heart was still racing and he was trying to rationalise his experience. He decided that he must have imagined the whole thing and put it down to working too hard. A few weeks past uneventfully, but one night Grahame was coming home through the woods when he came across the ghost of Anne Walker once more. This time she was much more forceful, but Grahame fled and, again, did not report the crime. Months passed, but these occurrences had adversely affected the miller, there were fears for his health and he was no longer the cheerful man he had previously been. Onlookers commented that he seemed to have the weight of the world upon his shoulders.

Just before Christmas that year Grahame was in his garden when Anne Walker appeared to him again, this time the demands were even more threatening. Grahame could no longer pretend that this was his imagination and he agreed to report the murder to the authorities.

The next day he went to the local magistrates and, after telling the full story, an immediate search of the pit was ordered. The decomposing body of Anne Walker was found and recovered from the pit. The pickaxe was also found under the bank, just as Anne had said, together with the bloodstained clothing.

John Walker and Mark Sharpe were subsequently arrested and charged with the murder of Anne Walker. Speculation was rife amongst the villagers as Walker was known to have abused his wife prior to her death, and his niece had become pregnant shortly after moving in with her uncle; she was asked but would not say who was responsible. Now it appeared that John Walker's motive for the killing of his niece was to hide the fact that he was indeed the father.

The trial of John Walker and Mark Sharpe took place in August 1631 at the Assizes Court on Durham Palace Green. Both men pleaded 'Not Guilty'.

The trial was ruled over by Judge Davenport, and one witness, a Mr Fairhair, swore under oath that he had seen the likeness of a child on John Walker's shoulders.

The jury found the prisoners to be guilty and Judge Davenport immediately passed the sentence of death on both men. John Walker and Mark Sharpe were hanged, but pleaded their innocence until their dying breath.

Visitor Information

Address:
Lumley Castle Hotel
Chester-le-Street
County Durham
DH3 4NX

Tel: 0191 3891111
Email: reservations@lumleycastle.com
Website: www.lumleycastle.com

How to Get There: Leave the A1(M) at junction 63. Take the turn off for Chester le Street and follow signs for Riverside. You will then pick up signs for Lumley Castle
OS Map Reference: NZ 287 510

Additional Information:
- Lumley Castle Hotel has seventy-three bedrooms including: Courtyard and Castle single and double bedrooms as well as Four Poster Feature and Executive bedrooms. The King James Suite is an exclusive suite which includes a 20ft high four-poster Queen Anne bed and an *en-suite* bathroom and jacuzzi with views over the surrounding parkland
- Lumley Castle has the capacity to host functions for up to 150, and can provide a bespoke service for meetings, seminars, product launches and team-building events. Wifi access is also free
- Lumley Castle is an idyllic setting for a wedding ceremony and reception. Please visit the website or contact the hotel for further information
- Regular events take place at Lumley Castle including murder mystery evenings, and Hallowe'en banquets. Please visit the hotel's website for more information
- Experience the superb food and elegant surroundings in the Black Knight Restaurant or in the comfort of your own exclusive dining room. Up-to-date menus and prices can be found on the hotel's website

The Manor House Hotel

*T*he Manor House was built at the end of the sixteenth century as a farmer's dwelling. The building has had a fairly unremarkable history, it changed hands a number of times and continued life as a domestic home. In 1913, the vicar of St Luke's Church, Revd Thomas Lomax, had the manor converted into an orphanage. A local doctor bought the building a few years later and it reverted back to a private home. In 1989 the building was sold again and the new owners opened the Manor House as a hotel.

Despite the quiet past of the Manor House Hotel, the building holds a number of frightening secrets and terrifying occurrences take place on an all too frequent basis. The most common sighting is of the full apparition of a tall woman seen on the staircase by visitors and more often by staff, who have nicknamed her Betty. Betty is often reported to be weeping and mediums have claimed that Betty is endlessly searching for her young child who vanished when she was working in the building. There have been skeletal remains of children and babies found buried in the hotel's garden and it is believed that one of these poor innocent children is Betty's missing child. Why the children are buried in the garden, and who or what killed them, is a mystery that may never be solved.

Visitors to Room 4 have complained of a strong smell of tobacco, most commonly in the early hours of the morning, usually between 3 a.m. and 4 a.m.

The owner's son claims to have seen the ghosts of children in Room 6; he says they tell him they want to play with him. He has said that they cover their eyes and count to ten and then they chase him. A dark figure has also been seen walking through Room 6 and on a number of occasions a child's crying has been heard in the middle of the night.

Visitors and members of staff have reported that Room 7 has felt very oppressive; this is followed by a dark shadow looking to resemble a heavy set, tall man, appearing in the corner of the room, never moving, then simply vanishing. With his disappearance, the oppressive atmosphere lifts.

One guest to Room 7, with no knowledge of the unusual happenings, had a lamp shade thrown at them; it missed them by inches. On a separate occasion a maid was in the bathroom cleaning when she was pushed hard in the back, upon

Manor House Hotel. (By kind permission of the Manor House Hotel)

turning around she found she was the only person in the room; she had locked the door behind her when she entered the room and it remained locked.

Room 8 has experienced some extreme poltergeist activity, dark shadows are commonly seen moving swiftly through the room, and during a séance night at the hotel a medium claimed that a murder had once taken place in the room.

The owner's son was asleep in bed in Room 8 when something grabbed him by the throat; he was then picked up and thrown from his bed. He ran downstairs in hysterics to see his mother. She initially assumed that it was all a bad dream; however, when she looked at his throat she was horrified to find bright red finger impressions. The little boy now won't go upstairs on his own; he sits at the bottom of the stairs waiting for an adult to go up with him.

All of the rooms in the hotel have had reports of televisions turning themselves on and off during the night. This was captured on film during the *Most Haunted* episode recorded at the Manor House Hotel.

Darren Ritson, paranormal investigator and author of a number of books on the subject, including *Ghost Hunter, Haunted Newcastle*, and co-author of *The South Shields Poltergeist*, investigated the Manor House Hotel in 2005:

*The corridor that runs outside of some of the hotel's most active rooms; Rooms 4, 6, and 7.
(By kind permission of the Manor House Hotel)*

Betty has been seen on these stairs. (By kind permission of the Manor House Hotel)

There have been skeletal remains of children found buried beneath the garden.
(By kind permission of the Manor House Hotel)

On Saturday the 17th Sept 2005, GHOST and a few selected guests carried out an investigation there and it has to be one of the most eventful I have attended to date as a ghost hunter. We arrived at about 8.30 p.m. on the night in question and were shown to the most haunted wing of the building: Rooms 7 and 8. We made ourselves comfortable and prepared for the night's investigation. We carried out baseline tests and then we set up a trigger object in Room 7 and a flour tray experiment in Room 8. A long, plastic tub of flour was placed on a sturdy surface and objects were placed into the flour. In this case we used crystals and a red lollipop as young spirit children allegedly frequent this area. By placing these objects into the tray and leaving the crucifix locked off in Room 7, we hoped we might achieve some spiritual interaction with these objects; ultimately they may be moved, indicating some form of ghostly presence. We then split into two groups and while Lee Stephenson, Suzanne Hitchinson, Fiona Vipond and I went to Room 8 to investigate, Drew Bartley and his group stayed in Room 7.

Our investigation began with us settling down, calling out to the atmosphere and asking for phenomena while at the same time recording it with my dictation machine. For a while nothing seemed to happen until quite a while into the vigil when we all

Room 7. (By kind permission of the Manor House Hotel)

started to hear the odd click, or tap. Some of the investigators also felt funny feelings, and the distinct smell of vomit was smelt by all at one point in the vigil; a commonly reported occurrence by all accounts.

After the split vigils, we all regrouped back in Room 8, where earlier on it had been reported that the beam barriers that were placed at the door had been turned around while the investigators were all sitting on the bed. It was there we decided to hold a séance. This, it seemed, was indeed the room to investigate thoroughly. We caught some light anomalies on the night vision video camera and there was a definite feeling of something, or someone around us; this was agreed by all present.

Drew and I monitored the séance proceedings while the rest of the group sat in the circle and conducted the séance. Prior to the séance beginning, a photograph was taken of the flour tray showing ten crystals, a red lollipop, and flat, undisturbed floor. When everyone was ready and comfortable, Suzanne proceeded to conduct the séance and it wasn't long before she was aware of spirit presences. She picked up on two children, a boy and a girl, and said they were related. Fiona then asked the children if they would like a lollipop. Fiona then said that 'they were welcome to take the one we had left as a trigger object in the flour.

After a minute or so, I shone my torch onto the flour tray to see if there had been any movement with our objects and I was not disappointed. I was stunned to see that the flour had indeed been disturbed, as if someone had literally dragged two or three of their fingers through the flour, leaving it piled up at one side of the tray, this flour had seriously been disturbed! But then the real shock came, as we all noticed the red lollipop had completely vanished from within the tray. It must be stressed that I was in fact monitoring the séance from that area so know no one had touched it. Drew was on the other side of the room and everyone else was sitting in the séance. So who took the lollipop? It could only have been one of the spirit children.

This was a first for us all, for all the trigger object experiments we have set up over the years, granted, some do indeed move from their positions but only slightly or an inch at the most, but this one had completely vanished and was taken away from under all our noses and was never seen again. I can assure you, no one touched the flour tray objects and everyone turned out their pockets and was checked for flour on their hands and clothes, just as a precautionary measure. Everyone was clean, but I knew this would be the case. It is also interesting to add that flour patches and flour stains were later found on the carpet near the room door, (this patch was the identical size and shape of the lollipop); we also found flour in the bathroom, outside on the landing and down the stairs in the corridor.

We can only conclude it was taken from the flour tray by the children said to haunt this area, out of the actual room, into the corridor and down the stairs. We all know that no one living had actually left the room while we were there. This incident baffled us all somewhat, and we were all convinced we had experienced true ghostly activity. We were so impressed, we spent the rest of the night talking it through and trying to locate the lollipop stick. We never found it. So, what a night of investigating we had. It certainly proved very interesting indeed.

Although the malevolent entity that is also said to reside in Room 8 did not manifest for us in the way we had hoped, the spirit children really did us proud.

Visitor Information

Address:
The Manor House Hotel
The Green
West Auckland
County Durham
DL14 9HW

Tel: 01388 834834
Email: enquiries@manorhousehotelcountydurham.co.uk
Website: www.manorhousehotel.net

How to Get There: The Manor House Hotel is on the A68, 8 miles from Junction 58 on the A1(M)
OS Map Reference: NZ 176 260

Additional Information:
- The hotel has thirty-five bedrooms, including executive and four-poster-bed rooms. Each room is equipped with tea and coffee-making facilities, flat screen digital television and telephone
- Guests are welcome to bring dogs for a £10 surcharge if staying in selected rooms; please mention this when booking
- All hotel guests can enjoy free use of the hotel's health club, with access to a swimming pool, spa bath, fitness suite, sauna, and vertical tanning booths
- Juniper Restaurant offers fine cuisine in delightful surroundings; a sample menu is available to view on the website. The Juniper Brasserie offers the same high quality food but in a more informal atmosphere
- Drinks are available in the Beehive Cocktail Lounge and adjoining Library
- The Knights Hall Suite is the ideal location for wedding receptions, catering for up to 120 guests. More information is available from the website, or by calling the hotel
- The Knights Hall Suite is also available for conferencing, as is the Eden Room, which can comfortably cater for eighteen delegates
- The Manor House Hotel regularly offer special deals on their website

The North of England Lead Mining Museum

*P*ark Level Mine opened in 1853 to explore the rich veins of lead ore found at Killhope. The moors and dales of the North Pennines echoed to the sound of the lead mining industry for over fifty years until the mine ceased to operate in 1910.

The miners were ill equipped to protect themselves from the threat of injury as a result of a falling object or explosions. There were three recorded deaths in Park Level, but hundreds more died as a result of Anthracosis, a lung disease caused by inhaling dust. The miners called the dreaded illness 'the Black Spit', and once they began to cough and spit a dark substance they knew death was sure to follow.

Children as young as seven were employed to work long hours on the Washing Floor for just fourpence a day, breaking up and separating the lead ore from the waste. This practice was replaced in the late 1870s when Park Level Mill was built. The mill utilised a waterwheel of 12m in diameter to crush up and separate the lead ore.

Park Level Mine reopened briefly during the First World War to supply the North East with much-needed lead.

Restoration of Killhope started in 1980, and today the North East Lead Mining Museum is the most complete lead mining museum in Britain. The famous Killhope Wheel was once one of many waterwheels in the area, but is now the only one to survive. Visitors have access to the grounds and can also go underground into Park Level Mine.

Belief that the mine, the grounds, and the surrounding woodland, are haunted date back to when it was still a working mine. The miners were convinced that ghosts walked at Killhope, and used to call them 'Tommy Knockers'. Some of these ghosts were benign spirits that meant no harm, but it was commonly accepted that there were a number of evil phantoms, intent on causing disruption and misery.

In more recent years, staff and visitors have experienced paranormal goings-on, including footsteps and hushed voices heard inside the mine shop when there's been no one there but the member of staff on duty. People on tours into the mine

Park Level Mill and the Killhope Wheel.
(By kind permission of the North of England Lead Mining Museum)

The entrance to Park Level Mine.
(By kind permission of the North of England Lead Mining Museum)

The Smithy. (By kind permission of the North of England Lead Mining Museum)

The Miner's Cottage. (By kind permission of the North of England Lead Mining Museum)

have felt as if someone else has been there; when they have mentioned it upon leaving the mine other people have described the same sensation. Glimpses of a dark shadowy figure have also been caught in the torchlight. It is believed that the phantom haunting the mine could be that of Thomas Heslop who died on 18 September 1879. He was caught inside a waterwheel and was torn limb from limb. Miners entering Park Level were horrified to find themselves walking not through the muddy water they would normally encounter, but blood, complete with body parts floating past them.

Perhaps the most unusual occurrence of all is to be found in the Miner's Cottage; the room is made up how it would have been during the days of the working mine, complete with mannequins. There is a draughts board in the room to demonstrate the type of pastimes the miners would have had, and staff have found that pieces move overnight when the museum is locked up and no one is on site.

There is a local legend of a woman who went into the woods late one night looking for her husband and was never seen again. It is unknown where this story originated from, or even what era it is believed to have taken place in. However, in the dead of night a woman's scream has been heard coming from the heavily wooded land.

I spoke to sports and celebrity psychic Dean 'Midas' Maynard (www.deanmidasmaynard.com) who led a paranormal investigation at the North of England Lead Mining Museum in 2003. He remembered it vividly, and told me it was the most terrifying night of his life:

We arrived at 9 p.m. and saw that the little hut that was our home for the night was surrounded by woods, with no street lighting, and the mine only had one road in and out. It was at this point that I realised for the one and only time in my paranormal career that I had severely underestimated the North of England Lead Mining Museum; it was dark, eerie and very foreboding.

The owner left us at 10 p.m. with matches and some coal and we were all alone for the night in the middle of nowhere.

The night started very quietly and around 1.30 a.m. we went for a walk in the woods. About 1 mile in we stumbled across a derelict cottage that had no windows and had clearly not been occupied for some time, the only way to describe it was it looked like a smaller version of the house at the end of the movie, *Blair Witch Project*.

We entered the cottage very nervously and lasted about two minutes as it had a very unnerving 'we were not alone' feeling to it.

As we started briskly walking back I heard a woman's shout coming back from the cottage, I kept it to myself as I thought it was just my imagination … it wasn't!

Ten seconds later my colleague confirmed this by shouting 'did you hear that woman shout?' We quickly walked back to the miner's hut on ground level to regroup and gather our composure. However, fifteen minutes later we were terrified once again as the side door suddenly began to rattle as if someone was trying to get in.

We finally left the museum at 3 a.m. as the cottage and door-rattling experience had genuinely shaken us up and we were beginning to see and hear all manner of ghostly goings-on all around us without being able to differentiate between our imagination and reality; I simply had to get out of there. The North of England Lead Mining Museum is still to this day the most unnerving investigation I have been involved with.

Visitor Information

Address:
The North of England Lead Mining Museum
Near Cowshill
Upper Weardale
County Durham
DL13 1AR

Tel: 01388 537505
Email: info@killhope.org.uk
Website: www.killhope.co.uk

Opening Hours:
1 April – 1 November, daily 10.30 a.m. – 5 p.m., last entry 4.30 p.m.
However, open all year for pre-booked groups of over ten people

How to Get There: The museum is in Upper Weardale, 8 miles from Alston, and can be located on the A689 Stanhope-Alston road. In summer, buses run by request from Stanhope to the mining centre. Call for further information on (0191) 3833337
OS Map Reference: NY 825 431

Additional Information:
- Guided tours into the mine run regularly throughout the day, with free hire of hard hat, waterproof boots, and torch
- A well-stocked gift shop, and a café selling hot food and drinks is located on site
- There is a woodland walk signposted through the haunted woodland surrounding the lead mine
- There is wheelchair access to some public areas, and wheelchairs are available for loan
- Education facilities are available and school groups are welcome. Please contact the museum for further information
- There are baby changing facilities
- Dogs are welcome

The Oak Tree Inn

*T*he Liddel family descends from Thomas Liddel, a wealthy merchant of Newcastle-upon-Tyne and loyal supporter of Charles I. In 1642 Charles I granted him the title of Baronet of Ravensworth Castle, which was to become the family seat. In 1690 Tantobie Manor was built in Stanley nearby for the 'lesser' members of the Liddel family, and was the first building of the village of Tantobie which developed around the manor.

In the mid-1800s the manor, which had been left empty for decades, was opened as the Oak Tree Inn, offering accommodation to travellers passing through, and a gathering place for the locals to enjoy a drink or a meal. Today, the Oak Tree Inn retains much of the original Victorian décor, and also features an open fire. The staff, owners and customers may have changed as the decades have passed, but one thing has remained constant: the Oak Tree Inn's resident ghosts.

The most regularly reported spirit is that of a man who sits silently on a corner seat, appearing to enjoy a drink, near to the open fire. He appears solid, and most witnesses could have easily mistaken him for a regular customer, except for his clothing which is eighteenth century in appearance and includes a tricorn hat.

The identity of this spirit is unknown, but he has been seen hundreds of times throughout the history of the inn. He has also been held responsible for the audible phenomena experienced at the Oak Tree Inn, from the radio in the bar being turned up and down, to footsteps heard coming from the room directly above the bar. On one such occasion in the 1970s the owner heard the footsteps and was convinced someone was upstairs, so gathered together several of the men drinking at the bar to accompany her upstairs to confront the intruder. However, there was no one there and all of the windows and doors were locked. As they wondered where the intruder could have gone, they heard the footsteps again, this time they were louder and were coming from the very room they were standing in. All of the group were standing perfectly still, but the footsteps could clearly be heard walking from one side of the room to the other before stopping as suddenly as they had begun.

The same spirit has also been blamed for playing practical jokes on men visiting the toilet. Male members of staff have found themselves unable to open the outer toilet door, pulling as hard as possible but unable to budge it. Then, after they have been trapped for a few minutes, it suddenly opens to reveal that no other member

The Oak Tree Inn. (By kind permission of the Oak Tree Inn)

The ghost of a man in eighteenth-century garb has been seen throughout the Oak Tree Inn.
(By kind permission of the Oak Tree Inn)

of staff or customer could have been holding the other side of the door. This was first reported in the winter of 1995, but has occurred regularly in the years that have followed.

The Oak Tree Inn's other ghostly resident is that of a small black cat. It has been seen, and heard, regularly. A number of customers over the years have apologised to the bar staff for letting the cat out when they came in. There have even been complaints from customers that cats should not be allowed in the inn after they've seen the spectral cat run behind the bar, or into the kitchen.

Visitor Information

Address:
The Oak Tree Inn
Front Street
Tantobie
Stanley
County Durham
DH9 9RF

Tel: 01207 235445

How to Get There: From A1(M) follow signs for A692 Consett, then after 8 miles follow the B6173 to Stanley. After 1 mile turn right
OS Map Reference: NZ 176 546

Additional Information:
- The Oak Tree Inn has five *en-suite* bedrooms; please contact the inn for booking information and availability. All rooms are furnished with colour television, hairdryer, tea and coffee-making facilities, and a telephone
- There is free car parking at the inn
- Food is available from the bar daily. Bookings can also be made for breakfast, evening meals, and lunch (Sunday lunch 12 noon – 6 p.m.)
- All major credit cards accepted
- The Oak Tree Inn can be hired for wedding receptions
- Pets are accepted to stay with guests

Preston Hall Museum

*P*reston Hall and the 100 acres of parkland that form Preston Park are found in the heavily wooded Tees Valley near Stockton. The earliest reference to the land, which was farmland at the time, was in 1183 in The Boldon Buke, County Durham's version of the Domesday Book.

The next recorded happening was in 1515; by this time a grand manor had been constructed and was in the ownership of William Sayer. However, the manor and surrounding grounds were lost when the estates of Lawrence Sayer, a Royalist in the English Civil War, were seized by the Crown.

George Witham purchased the manor in 1673 and it was renamed Witham Hall. In 1722 William Witham sold the estate to Sir John Eden of Windlestone and in 1812 it was sold to David Burton Fowler. It was David Burton Fowler who, in 1825, commenced the construction of Preston Hall as it stands today.

Local shipbuilder Robert Ropner bought the Hall in 1882 and held on to it until after the Second World War, when plans were drawn up to turn Preston Park into a shopping centre. However, the estate was bought by Stockton Borough Council and in 1953 Preston Hall was opened to the public as a museum and gallery.

In the years that have passed since the museum opened, visitors and staff have reported an extraordinary number of unusual occurrences.

The ghost of a highwayman has been witnessed outside the front entrance to the museum. It is believed that he may have worked the Stockton & Darlington Railway, which runs just behind Preston Park. His identity remains a mystery, as is when, and how, he died. Psychic mediums who have visited Preston Hall Museum have failed to pick on any information relating to the highwayman.

Preston Hall's Grey Lady is the best known spectral resident of the museum. She has been seen in the 'Brown Corridor' (which is the name often given to the corridor which runs past the Period Rooms). Visitors in this corridor have inexplicably felt a great sorrow, often beginning to cry themselves. A medium who visited the museum explained that the tragic young lady behind the mystery of the Grey Lady once lived at the Hall. She fell pregnant to the groundsman, later losing the baby. An alternative explanation was offered by an historian to the museum in the early 1990s. He told of a son of the family living at the manor who fell in love with a local peasant girl. However, the family saw the girl as being beneath their son and

Preston Hall Museum. (By kind permission of Preston Hall Museum)

forbade him from seeing her again. Heartbroken, the young girl walked into the middle of Preston Park and killed herself. Which of these stories is more accurate, and, more importantly, the true identity of the Grey Lady, may never be known.

In an area of the museum known as the Dungeon (which is actually an old wine cellar) a dog has been seen to walk through a wall. People often feel very uncomfortable in the Dungeon and some visitors have struggled to spend more than a few minutes in the room, commonly describing the sensations of fear, terror, and foreboding.

A ghostly cleaner polishes display cases throughout the museum, and the spirit of a First World War soldier has been seen on the Armoury stairs.

Northern Ghost Investigations arranged a ghost hunt at Preston Hall Museum in February 2008 to raise funds for the Butterwick Hospice. Claire Robinson was part of the NGI team that attended and she told me of what lay in wait for them that evening at Preston Hall Museum:

> As soon as we entered the room with the famous Georges de la Tour painting (The Dice Players), my breathing became shallow and fast. I could find no reason for this; I didn't feel out of breath and had not exerted myself in any way prior to entering the room. The room felt full of energy. I went to see if the medium in our party was picking up anything and straight away I noticed his breathing had altered also. He said he sensed several energies in here, one of which was very strong.

We seated ourselves around the room and then several guests began to complain of differing sensations including stomach pains, pressure in the ear similar to the 'popping' experienced at high altitudes, and heaviness and pressure like the last few weeks of pregnancy. Several mediums, including Ian Lawman and Ralph Keeton who were present that evening, have picked up on a pregnant woman at Preston Hall who has a tragedy surrounding her and her unborn child.

A guest suggested using a pendulum, so we got her to stand in the centre of the room where the medium sensed the energy was strongest. The pendulum began to swing from side to side while questions were asked of the spirits present. It continued to swing for almost forty-five minutes before stopping suddenly. One of the investigators was using a laser thermometer to record the temperature in the room, and the pendulum stopped at exactly the same time as a drastic drop in the room temperature. The pendulum started swinging again rapidly, then after thirty seconds stopped dead instantly. During this time the temperature changes became erratic, rising as the pendulum was swinging then dropping at the point that it stopped. This happened four times before the temperature became constant and the pendulum stopped swinging completely.

Our group of ten investigators made our way to our next location, the Toy Room. The room didn't 'feel' haunted and we were all quite at ease. We decided to create an energy circle to see if we could pick up on any spirits that may have been present. At first we had some teething problems as I had to break the circle several times to redirect lost guests from other groups who had wandered up by mistake, but eventually we began. After a fairly long period of time with no success, the exercise became light-hearted and some of the guests to the investigation got the giggles. We felt comfortable in the Toy Room, and all felt fairly confident that if the room is haunted, that we were not in the company of anything 'otherworldly'. A member of another group came to join us but fell over in the darkness which had us all in fits of laughter. However, laughter turned to terror as simultaneously every mobile phone in the room began to ring and beep. Everyone was immediately stunned, or scared, into complete silence. Four of the team confirmed that their phone had been turned off, and all of the other mobiles were on silent, something we ask of everyone at the beginning of every investigation. I cannot see any rational explanation for this occurrence.

Claire went on to tell me of her run, in with the Grey Lady during a visit to Preston Hall in her childhood:

When I was a child we came to Preston Hall on a primary school visit. We had some free time near the end of our trip to explore the Hall on our own. My best friend and I went back to the corridor with all the rooms made up in period style. We had enjoyed this area the most because we thought it was spooky. We were the only visitors in this part of the Hall and we both saw something which caused us to scream in terror and flee.

The Brown Corridor. (By kind permission of Preston Hall Museum)

I'm a bit hazy with what exactly it was we saw specifically; however, I know it was an older lady wearing an old-fashioned long dress, who we suddenly seemed to perceive as a ghost and a 'threat'. We both saw this at exactly the same time and we both reacted at the same time. We got into trouble with our teacher and were told we had made the whole thing up. On and off over the years I've always wondered about this, as the feelings of menace and terror from 'it' were very vivid, yet I've always thought that maybe we did make it up, or at least see something normal which scared us, despite my memories of the incident. It was only on a visit to the museum with my own daughter about three years ago, when I spoke to a member of staff who told me of an apparition that he and a colleague encountered. What he described in great detail was exactly the same thing I had seen all those years earlier.

Visitor Information

Address:
Preston Hall Museum and Park
Yarm Road
Eaglescliffe
Stockton-on-Tees
TS18 3RH

Tel: 01642 527375
Email: prestonhall@stockton.gov.uk
Website: www.stockton.gov.uk/museums

Opening Hours:
Monday – Friday 10 a.m. – 4.30 p.m.
Saturday – Sunday 11 a.m. – 4.30 p.m.
Last admission 4 p.m.

How to Get There: The museum is situated on the A135 (Yarm Road). The museum is well signposted
OS Map Reference: NZ 429 157

Additional Information:
- There is a gift shop at the museum
- There is a restaurant serving hot and cold food
- For school, workshop, or group bookings telephone 01642 527375
- Baby changing facilities are available
- Audio guides specifically for blind and partially sighted visitors are available. There are also Touch exhibits
- Wheelchair access to some public areas and wheelchairs are available for hire

Raby Castle

The name Raby is of Viking origin and means 'Settlement on the Boundary'. In the eleventh century King Cnut, the Viking King of England, Denmark and Norway, owned a mansion on the site where Raby Castle stands today. Cnut handed the estate back to the Northumbrian Bishops of Durham as a gesture of goodwill, the lands having been taken from the Northumbrians in the late ninth century by Viking invaders.

The land was passed into the hand of the Nevilles, an influential Norman family, and it was John, 3rd Baron Neville, who was responsible for building the castle in around 1360, with Bulmer Tower incorporating the only remains of Cnut's mansion. John obtained a Licence to Crenellate in 1378, allowing him to add fortifications to the building.

In 1569, 700 men gathered in the Barons Hall to plot the infamous 'Rising of the North', led by two members of the great Northern nobility: Charles Neville, 6th Earl of Westmoreland, and Thomas Percy, 7th Earl of Northumberland. At the time, much of the North followed Catholicism and the rebels wished to depose Elizabeth I and replace her with her Catholic cousin, Mary Queen of Scots. The rebellion failed and Raby Castle, along with the Nevilles' other estates, were seized by the Crown.

The castle remained in the possession of the Crown until 1626 when Sir Henry Vane the Elder, Treasurer to Charles I, bought Raby Castle to be the seat of his family.

The year 1641 saw the beginning of the Civil War, which lasted a decade, and the castle was attacked by Royal forces on five occasions. Raby suffered considerable damage but the castle was repaired swiftly.

The castle passed from generation to generation, and a vast number of changes have taken place down the centuries, resulting in the magnificent palatial property that stands today as one of the largest inhabited castles in England. The current owner, Lord Barnard, is a direct descendent of the Vane family.

Raby Castle looks every bit the archetypal haunted castle, and does not disappoint. It is reputed to be haunted by the spirits of three of Raby's previous inhabitants. The most commonly reported sighting is that of the ghost of Charles Neville, which is often seen in the Barons Hall, re-enacting the plotting of the

Raby Castle. (By kind permission of Raby Castle)

'Rising of the North'. He has also been witnessed ascending the staircase which leads to the hall.

Henry Vane the Younger, son of Sir Henry Vane the Elder, is another phantom who has been seen at Raby Castle by a number of terrified visitors. In life Henry was a vociferous activist and was imprisoned in the Tower of London for high treason. He was placed on trial and sentenced to be beheaded.

He was executed on Tower Hill on the 14 June 1662. A large crowd gathered and Henry took out a small piece of paper and began to make his final speech. All attempts to interrupt him failed so the sheriff instructed trumpeters to drown out his voice. Undaunted, he continued to make his speech until the fatal blow struck his neck and his head dropped into the basket.

Henry's headless ghost is seen at the library at Raby Castle, his body seated, and his head before him upon a desk, his lips moving, but no sound being heard – as if he is still trying to make his final speech.

The final ghostly resident at Raby Castle is that of the first Lady Barnard, known as 'Old Hell Cat' due to her explosive temper. Lord and Lady Barnard disapproved strongly of their son Gilbert's fiancée and begged him not to marry her, considering the woman to be beneath Gilbert. The marriage went ahead and Gilbert's parents were furious. His father, Lord Barnard, was so angry that he tried to destroy Raby Castle, so Gilbert and his wife would find the castle to be of little worth when they inherited it. He stripped lead from the roof, ripped up floors, felled trees, and even killed every single one of the deer in the park. Only a lawsuit stopped the castle being damaged further, and Lord Barnard was ordered to pay for all repairs.

Lady Barnard is still angry in death with her son for his defiance and is seen walking the halls after dark, her eyes glowing as she knits with white hot knitting needles.

The area surrounding Raby Castle is also believed to be haunted, possibly more so than the castle. Mary Ann Cotton was a serial killer living in the area in the nineteenth century; she murdered three husbands, her lover, a friend, her own mother, and twelve of her children, making all of the deaths appear to be from gastric fever. She was eventually found out and hanged at Durham County Gaol on 24 March 1873. The ghosts of her twelve murdered children are said to play a ghoulish game of follow-my-leader through the fields and wooded areas around the castle.

Visitor Information

Address:
Raby Castle
Staindrop
Darlington
County Durham
DL2 3AH

Tel: 01833 660202
Email: admin@rabycastle.com
Website: www.rabycastle.com

Opening Hours:
Easter weekend Saturday – Monday Park and Gardens: 11 a.m. – 5.30 a.m., Castle:
1 p.m. – 5 p.m.
May, June and September, Sunday – Wednesday Park and Gardens: 11 a.m. – 5.30
p.m., Castle: 1 p.m. – 5 p.m.
July and August, daily except Saturdays Park and Gardens: 11 a.m. – 5.30 p.m.,
Castle: 1 p.m. to 5 p.m.
Bank Holiday Weekends also open Saturdays

How to Get There: Off the A688, 2 miles north of Staindrop
OS Map Reference: NZ 125 221

Additional Information:
- The castle caters for tours and groups, including educational visits. Please visit the castle's website for more information
- A full-colour guidebook is on sale at the castle
- The licensed Stable Tearooms, which incorporate the stalls of the eighteenth-century stables, provides a tranquil setting for light lunches, afternoon teas and snacks. Reservations can be made in advance for groups
- Overnight ghost hunts are not permitted at Raby Castle
- Wheelchair access is limited to some of the ground floor, the gardens are accessible but the gravel path can pose difficulties for unaccompanied wheelchair users
- Baby changing facilities are available in both the male and female toilets
- Dogs are not allowed in the castle and gardens, except guide/assistance dogs
- Photography and video filming is not permitted inside the castle

Redworth Hall Hotel

Redworth Hall is a stunning Jacobean country house dating back to 1693. Little is recorded of its early history, but by the year 1740 the building had been abandoned. Robert Surtees acquired the old manor house and estate at Redworth and carried out extensive rebuilding work in 1744, incorporating some of the seventeenth-century fabric. A Great Hall was built, as well as a wonderful ornate staircase. He created a grand mansion two storeys high to which his nephew and heir, also Robert Surtees, added further improvements in 1820.

The Surtees family lived at Redworth Hall until Henry Surtees passed away in 1955. The building was then used as a school before being converted into a luxury hotel. Today, Redworth Hall Hotel is certainly a beautiful building, with almost 100 lavishly decorated bedrooms, two restaurants, and a health and leisure club. However, after dark the hotel takes on a completely different appearance; surrounded by 150 acres of woodland and moorland the remote location is extremely unsettling. The floorboards are ominously creaky and it comes as no surprise to some guests to find out that the hotel is haunted by a number of ghosts.

The land on which Redworth Hall was built was the site on which many battles took place during the English Civil War; many people lost their lives here and some of the violent poltergeist activity within the cellar of the hotel has been attributed to this. Footsteps have been heard by terrified members of staff when no one else has been in the cellar at the time. A team of paranormal investigators were in the cellar in July 2007, and one investigator narrowly avoided injury when a glass was thrown across the room, missing his head by inches. Candles and stones were also thrown, followed by the door opening and slamming shut on demand.

The Great Hall is believed to be haunted by the spirit of a young girl. It is unknown who she is, or why she haunts this particular room. Many people have witnessed the hazy figure of her standing before them motionless, then simply fading away. Other guests have felt someone tugging at their clothes and when they turned around found that there was no one there.

One of the spirits that remains at Redworth Hall Hotel has been identified as one of the Lord Surtees, although we're not sure of a first name. He was the owner of the estate during the late eighteenth century. He was a cruel man. He had a mentally handicapped son and resented his son for being born this way. He would never let

Redworth Hall Hotel at dusk. (Photograph provided courtesy of Redworth Hall Hotel)

him step foot outside of the Hall due to the shame he felt, and he would chain his son by his neck to the fireplace in the Great Hall. The spirit of Lord Surtees has been experienced throughout the Hall, as have the cries of anguish of his son, who died before his twentieth birthday, having never experienced the outside world.

There is another ghost at Redworth Hall Hotel with links to the same Lord Surtees: the ghost of a pretty young scullery maid who had an affair with Surtees, perhaps foolishly believing that he loved her the same way that she loved him. She fell pregnant and it was not long before Surtees' wife found out. Within a week the scullery maid was found dead at the foot of the ornate staircase. It was said

The Great Hall. (By kind permission of Redworth Hall Hotel)

she committed suicide by throwing herself down the stairs, but murder by Lord Surtees, his wife, or the pair of them, seems much more likely.

Guests staying in Room 9 have awoken in the early hours of the morning, commonly between 2 a.m. and 3 a.m., to see a dark figure standing at the bottom of the bed watching them sleep. As soon as a light is turned on by the panicked guest, the figure vanishes. Some guests have been so frightened that they have packed up their belongings and left in the middle of the night, rather than risk trying to go back to sleep in Room 9.

Visitor Information

Address:
Redworth Hall Hotel
Redworth
Darlington
County Durham
DL5 6NL

Tel: 01388 770600
Email: redworthhall@barcelo-hotels.co.uk
Website: www.barcelo-hotels.co.uk/hotels/northern-england/barcelo-redworth-hall-hotel/

How to Get There: From Junction 58 of the A1(M) take the A68 towards Corbridge. At the first roundabout take the second exit onto the A6072 towards Bishop Auckland. At the second roundabout again take the second exit
OS Map Reference: NZ 241 230

Additional Information:
- There is a wide variety of rooms to choose from, ranging from a standard twin, up to a Superior Deluxe. Further information on all rooms, including prices, can be found on the hotel's website
- Dining is available for residents and non-residents in Restaurant 1744 where you can enjoy a selection of traditional and contemporary dishes using seasonal and local produce. A full menu and pricing can be found on the website
- The award-winning Health & Leisure Club is located on the first floor of Barceló Redworth Hall and is free to use for guests staying at the hotel
- Redworth Hall Hotel is the perfect location to get married, whether it be a small intimate reception, or a larger grand affair. Call the hotel's wedding coordinators on 01388 770600

Walworth Castle

The construction of Walworth Castle was completed in 1189 by the Hansard family. The family, known as the Handsome Hansards, had begun the development of the castle, the estate, and a surrounding village in around 1150, choosing a site in the rolling countryside of the Tees valley. In charters dating back to the twelfth century, the castle is referred to by the name of Waleberge Castle, meaning 'a settlement of the Welsh'.

The Black Death struck England in the summer of 1349. The Black Death was the deadliest pandemic in human history and it killed almost 40 per cent of the population of England, around 2 million people. The country's recovery was hindered by successive waves of the plague and raids upon the North by the Scots. Walworth Castle had been the seat of the Hansard family for almost 200 years, but by the time the Black Death had subsided in 1350, history records that the castle and its estates had passed into the hands of others.

By 1391 the castle was bought back into the Hansard family, with Robert Hansard reclaiming the castle for his fourteen-year-old son, Richard. The castle had previously been held by Ralph Neville since 1367.

The castle remained in the family until 1539, when Elizabeth Hansard married Sir Francis Ayscough. Elizabeth gave birth to their only child, William Ayscough, and when his mother passed away in 1558, and his father in 1563, he inherited Walworth Castle.

William lived at Walworth with his wife until 1579, when the castle and all of its estates were sold to Thomas Jennison, an Auditor General who lived and worked in Ireland until his death in 1586. Elizabeth Jennison lived at Walworth Castle after the passing of her husband, and continued the restructuring of the castle that Thomas had instructed prior to his death.

In 1605 Elizabeth Jennison died and her son, William Jennison 'the Elder', inherited the estate. However, he never lived at Walworth Castle. He was imprisoned in 1610, and again in 1612, for being a Roman Catholic and for refusing to take an oath of allegiance to the Crown. The family suffered financially and incurred substantial debts. Without the necessary money to maintain Walworth Castle it began to decay and fall into ruin.

The decay of Walworth Castle continued with the succession of Jennisons who owned the estate during the years that followed. This was to change when

Walworth Castle. (By kind permission of Walworth Castle Hotel)

ten-year-old Ralph Jennison inherited the estate in 1704. Ralph became a Member of Parliament for Northumberland in 1727 and again in 1734. He restored the dilapidated building to its former glory, and carried out extensive redecoration throughout the castle. The decorative ceilings, doors, and windows chosen by Ralph can still be seen today in the reception, staircase, Hansard's Restaurant, and the Ballroom.

When Ralph died in 1759, his widow sold the castle for £16,000 to Matthew Stephenson, a wine merchant from Newcastle. He sold it on shortly afterwards to John Harrison. When John died in 1819 it was left to his only child, Ann Harrison. Ann married General Arthur Aylmer and it remained in the Aylmer family until 1931.

During the Second World War the castle was let to the Durham Light Infantry as an Officer's Mess and HQ. It was also used to hold high-ranking German officers. In 1950, Durham County Council bought Walworth Castle from two brothers, Charles and Neville Eade who had bought the castle following the death of the last Aylmer, and it was turned into a girls' boarding school.

Walworth Castle after dark. (Photograph supplied courtesy of Walworth Castle Hotel)

In 1981 the castle was renovated and converted into a luxury hotel. Walworth Castle Hotel remains one of the county's finest historic hotels to this day.

It appears that over 800 years of history have left a lasting impression on the building, as ever since the hotel first opened its doors ghostly happenings have been commonplace.

There is a legend of a maidservant becoming pregnant during an affair with one of the Lords of the estate. When he found out, he was furious and became worried about his reputation should anyone else discover the affair. He was having some work carried out on the castle so had her bricked up alive behind a wall where a spiral staircase had previously been. She was absolutely frantic, unable to see or move, screaming out for help and scratching at the walls in vain. Although her screams of terror will have undoubtedly been heard, no one came to her aid. It's unknown how long it took for her to die, but she, along with her unborn child, died behind that wall and her spirit remains at Walworth Castle to this very day. Her footsteps can still be heard climbing a staircase which no longer exists. She is also seen throughout the castle, often by guests who awaken to find a dark female figure standing watching them sleep.

The Jennison Suite is very active, with unusual sounds and objects moving on their own all too common. One day, in recent years, a cleaner was tidying the room when a cabinet moved on its own in front of the door blocking her only way out of the room.

It is believed that peasants working in the dungeon during a civil revolt tried to escape down a tunnel but were caught and punished. This is said to be the cause of the unusual sounds that have been heard, described as the moaning of someone in pain. Members of staff have also been pushed by unseen hands whilst in the Dungeon.

Another paranormal hotbed of activity is the corridor that runs past Room 17; footsteps are regularly heard and icy blasts, even on warm summer days, have been reported. One chambermaid even had her pigtails playfully tugged but when she turned around there was no one in the corridor with her. Mediums to Walworth Castle have said that this disturbance is the result of a spirit called Ralph. There have been three Ralphs associated with the castle during its history, but it is believed that this particular spirit is that of Ralph Jennison, who took over as owner of Walworth Castle aged only ten, and lived here for over fifty years. He is unable to rest due to the guilt he feels for taking his own brother's life in a tragic moment of madness. The pair were arguing outside the castle when things got heated and Ralph pulled out his pistol and shot his own brother in the chest. He suddenly realised what he had done and panic set in; he picked up his brother, who was badly bleeding but still conscious, and raced into the castle and up to the room which is now Room 17. He tended to his brother's wound but his brother slipped in and out of consciousness before closing his eyes one last time and slipping away into death. Ralph has never been able to forgive himself and remains at Walworth Castle for all eternity.

I spoke with Andrew Marsay who has investigated Walworth Castle several times in his role as Director of Paranormal Tours (www.paranormaltours.com), and he told me of the extraordinary phenomena he has encountered:

I stumbled across this location back in 2004 when researching locations for Paranormal Tours to investigate. I spoke to the owner and asked if he had had any recent reports of activity and he said that he and his staff had indeed had some unexplained happenings recently and over the past few years. I decided that it warranted further investigation and agreed to meet with the owner and perform an assessment of the site. As Walworth was about 300 miles from my home in Hampshire, my wife, son and I decided to make a little break out of our trip and booked a room at the castle.

On arriving we quickly checked into Room 17, opposite the Jennison Suite. My research had already flagged up some interesting happenings in the Jennison Suite but nothing about the room that we were staying in. After our long journey we ventured down to the restaurant, had a lovely meal, and then went back to the room to put our then one-year-old son to bed. I decided to set a little experiment up in our room.

By the door I rigged up one of our Negative Ion Detectors (NID) and also drew around three coins on a white sheet of paper. A 2p, 10p and £1 coin, so we had three different colours and sizes. The NID is a piece of kit that sends out an audible beep when it detects static electricity. The theory around using a NID on an investigation is that it is a possibility that when a 'spirit' enters our atmosphere it leaves a static trail behind it and the box indicates its presence.

It was just gone 3 a.m. when I woke up, hearing an intermittent beep from the NID. I couldn't see anything in the room however it distinctly felt like someone was watching us, or was it just my mind kicking in? After five minutes or so I rolled over and went back to sleep. In the morning when we got up I ventured over to the coin trigger object and was very surprised to see that the 10p had been completely moved out of its circle that I had drawn around. The two other coins were unaffected. I have no explanation as to why the NID went off nor why the 10p piece had been moved out from the circle. My wife hadn't done it, nor my son as he was fast asleep in his travel cot which he couldn't get out of without help from an adult.

Andrew went on to tell me that he definitely thought Walworth Castle Hotel was a worthy location for Paranormal Tours to investigate further, and it certainly did not disappoint:

I was sat with a group of investigators in the 'Morning Room' turret. It used to have a spiral staircase in there; however, today it is a circular room with a round table. We decided that it was an opportune moment to conduct a séance and all held hands asking out for any energies that were listening and happy to communicate to come forward. After fifteen minutes or so we noticed that the temperature in the room had dropped dramatically. Our laser temperature guns confirmed this. As we sat there, asking out, we all noticed that the room was getting noticeably darker along with the cold. It was after this that a strange white smoky mist appeared hovering above us, showing itself in the darkness. This mist thickened and became a swirling mass, still placed above us, then it suddenly dissipated in an instant. We all saw this whilst sat in our séance, not one of the team had a logical explanation as to what this mysterious mist actually was and how it came to disappear.

Visitor Information

Address:
Walworth Castle Hotel
Walworth
Darlington
DL2 2LY

Tel: 01325 485470
Email: enquiries@walworthcastle.co.uk
Website: www.walworthcastle.co.uk

How to Get There: From the A1(M) follow the A68 for 3 miles to Walworth
OS Map Reference: NZ 233 189

Additional Information:
- All thirty-four bedrooms have their own individual character, with many having their own uniquely designed upholstery. There are virtual tours of all the rooms on the castle's website. Bookings can be made by telephone or on online
- The award-winning Hansard's Restaurant offers contemporary dishes served in a traditional setting. Hansard's Library Tower is available for an intimate meal for two, or small family gatherings. Alternatively, the Farmers Bar is a traditional English pub well known for its carvery served daily
- Walworth Castle Hotel is the perfect setting for weddings. Contact the hotel for more information or to request a brochure
- Walworth Castle Hotel caters for conferencing and social events. Further information is available on the hotel's website

Whitworth Hall Hotel

*I*n 1183 Hugh du Puiset, the Bishop of Durham, ordered the compilation of the Boldon Buke. It has been called the 'Domesday Book of the North', and was designed to assist the administration of the vast diocesan estates. The estate of Whitworth was included and the entry read 'Thomas de Acle holds Whitworth for the free service of a quarter of a knight's fee'.

Thomas de Acle and his descendants were known as the Lords of Whitworth and would own the estate of Whitworth, which at the time was roughly 4 square miles, for the next three centuries. It's likely that Thomas de Acle's son, also called Thomas, may have built the first dwelling on the site where the hotel now stands in around 1260.

Thomas Whitworth, the last Lord of Whitworth, inherited the estate on 10 November 1355, aged thirteen. He went overseas to war in 1373, fighting in Spain and France before returning home many years later. He died childless and what happened after his death has been lost to history, as Whitworth is mentioned no more until 1420, by which time it was the possession of the Neville family.

The Nevilles held the Whitworth estate until 1569, when it became forfeited to the Crown on account of their involvement in the 'Rising of the North', an unsuccessful plot by the Catholics of Northern England against Elizabeth I.

In 1652 the manor at Whitworth was purchased by Mark Shafto, a lawyer from Newcastle-upon-Tyne. For over 300 years, twelve successive Shafto generations lived at Whitworth, the most notable being Robert Shafto, better known as 'Bonny' Bobby Shafto.

The Shafto family had seats at Bavington Hall, Beamish Hall, and Windlestone Hall, as well as Whitworth. Bobby held the manor at Whitworth from 1742 to 1797. In 1760, at the age of thirty, Bobby was elected MP for Durham City, a position he held for eight years after which he was succeeded by Sir Thomas Clavering. Bobby Shafto died in November 1797 and is buried in the Shafto family crypt beneath the floor of the Whitworth Church.

The Shaftos had turned Whitworth Hall into one of the finest family mansions in England, but it was largely destroyed by fire in 1876, with only the library and the kitchens being saved. The building lay in ruins until 1891 when the original three-storey hotel was rebuilt as the current two-storey building.

Whitworth Hall Hotel. (By kind permission of Whitworth Hall Hotel)

Whitworth Hall was sold by the Shafto family in October 1981 to a Mr Pamaby and it remained as a private dwelling until 1997, at which point it was sold again and the Grade II Listed Hall was converted into Whitworth Hall Hotel.

One of the oldest parts of the building, the library, is now the Library Restaurant and is a hive of paranormal activity. A man has been seen sitting at a table in the corner of the restaurant; he appears solid but vanishes when approached. Books have also fallen off shelves in the room, on one occasion striking a guest on the head. The corridor leading to the restaurant is also believed to be haunted, and staff have reported that at times it will inexplicably go so cold that you can see your own breath.

Room 6 appears to be a standard hotel room, lacking a remarkable or bloody history, yet staff feel uneasy in Room 6 and are reluctant to go in the room alone. Unusual sounds have been heard by guests in the early hours of the morning, reported to sound like coughing, or choking coming from under the bed.

In the Whitworth Suite, staff members working alone have been horrified to hear the silence broken by footsteps walking through the room, before stopping as suddenly as they began.

'Bonny' Bobby Shafto. (Image supplied courtesy of Whitworth Hall Hotel)

The Library Restaurant. (By kind permission of Whitworth Hall Hotel)

Lee Foster of www.hauntedland.co.uk spent a night at Whitworth Hall Hotel in June 2007 as a guest of Northern Ghost Investigations. He told me of what he encountered in one area of the hotel that is not usually associated with ghostly happenings – the vault:

The investigation of Whitworth Hall had been a disappointment in all of the rooms we'd spent time in. When we heard about the activity various staff had experienced over the years, the bar had been set and I'd hoped to meet or exceed this. The night seemed long during the paranormal void, even though my team had tried to coax activity through various communication methods such as calling out, table tipping, séance, and divination — all with a heavy dose of patience and all fruitless. I wanted to go back down to the vault, as Whitworth Hall, for me, 'felt' empty. This feeling trickled through the team as I sought out their views.

After what seemed like an age it was finally time for my team to visit the vault. Before entering I had another look around outside. I loved the sound of the night wind as it rustled the old, tall trees, and the fox calls, their screams lost in the darkness, were eerily like a human's cry of distress. An old derelict water mill was nearby, so I had a quick look around it. The shallow river, a mere trickle of its former self, was no longer powerful enough to turn the large, rusted water wheel or drive the seized-up cogs and gears inside the small, dark decrepit building. I felt quite sad to see that this little hidden treasure had become lost and irrelevant in the undergrowth. After I'd taken a few photographs I headed down the steps into the single-roomed, underground vault that lay only a few metres away.

The temperature inside was mild. Water slowly dripped from the roof and splashed onto the damp floor with an irregular drip, drip, drip. Two fluorescent lights brightly flooded the vault while the team settled into place. At one end of the vault, a staircase rose up into the darkness and, after a dozen steps, was sealed off by the courtyard above. Presumably these stairs would have led up into a building from long ago, possibly the original Whitworth Hall.

The Whitworth Suite. (By kind permission of Whitworth Hall Hotel)

I set my camcorder up in the far corner of the vault while the rest of the team stood quietly and took in the atmosphere. I could hear nervous chatter while I prepared myself for this location. For the first time tonight, I finally found my senses, and for the first time on an investigation, I felt on edge. I stood at the bottom of the dark staircase and hoped that this location would make up for the lack of activity we'd endured so far. When the bright lights were extinguished, darkness rushed in and swallowed us.

Pam, the team sensitive, called out for a spirit to come forth. She suggested that it could come down the stairs and touch one of us or show itself. In the darkness of the vault, I looked at the even darker void of the staircase beside me and suddenly I felt very unwelcome. A sense of foreboding pierced me from the cold, damp staircase. It was as if something had come down the stairs to find intruders in the room and [was] its anger emanated from the dark like a wave of fury. It was just as I sensed this and about to speak, that Pam looked as though she was pushed. She grabbed fellow team member Bruce to steady herself. It happened again and Pam asked whatever might be there to stop pushing her. Bruce spoke calmly and explained why we were in the vault. Seconds ticked slowly by. I could see Pam, Bruce, and the two guests dimly picked out in the emergency light, huddled close together. A feeling of anger hung in the air.

The sceptic in me searched for a reason. Autosuggestion, imagination, whatever caused this feeling was quite powerful as everyone in the room appeared on edge. So I reached my hand into the dark void of the stairwell and asked for whatever may be there to take it. The atmosphere appeared to change from one of anger to one of silent contemplation. I had hoped that something would grab my hand but at the same time wondered what I'd do if something did. The atmosphere continued to lighten but the darkness did not relinquish any secrets and after a few minutes the team decided to call an end to this location, much to the guests' relief. We had only spent a total of fifteen minutes in the vault, but for me it was the best part of the night. The lights chased away the darkness ready for the next team and we continued to our next location.

Personally, the vault was only place where I felt I had got something that questioned my scepticism. The other locations gave me nothing, but that's not to say that other people on other occasions don't get anything. Like a lot of things when it comes to the paranormal, it is a personal experience.

The NGI team felt that a number of unusual things occurred during the night between the various small teams and locations, but the spirits were not playing with us on this night. Was my experience real? I don't know. It felt real, but as always when you look back, and time blurs the memory, you try to rationalise it, which in turn makes the experience feel less real and [makes you wonder] did it actually happen?

Visitor Information

Address:
Whitworth Hall Hotel
Whitworth Hall Hotel Country Park
Spennymoor
County Durham
DL16 7QX

Tel: 01388 811772
Website: www.whitworthhall.co.uk

How to Get There: From the A1 join the A688 signposted towards Spennymoor, when you near Whitworth Hall Hotel follow the brown signs
OS Map Reference: NZ 234 347

Additional Information:
- There are twenty-nine bedrooms; all feature *en-suite* bathroom, free Wifi internet access, direct dial telephone, television, trouser press, hair dryer, and iron and ironing board. There are also four Premier Rooms which can have either a whirlpool bath or a four-poster bed
- Whitworth offers dining in the Silver Buckles Brasserie or the Library Restaurant, please contact the hotel, or visit the website for up-to-date serving times, prices, and menu options
- Whitworth Hall can offer conferencing facilities for anything between 2 and 250 people
- Whitworth Hall Hotel is a first-class venue for wedding ceremonies, receptions, celebrations and renewal of vows throughout the year. Please visit the hotel's website for further information
- Coarse fishing is permitted on the hotel's well-stocked lake. Day tickets can be purchased from the hotel
- The hotel's beautiful deer park is open daily and you can hand-feed the deer, with deer food being available to buy from the hotel

About the Author

Rob Kirkup was born in Ashington, Northumberland in 1979. He developed a keen interest in the paranormal from an early age, amassing a large collection of books and newspaper cuttings on the subject, and in particular stories of supernatural happenings in the North East of England.

In 2002, Rob led a paranormal investigation at Talkin Tarn, a haunted lake in Cumbria, as part of Alan Robson's Night Owls' Halloween show on Metro Radio. In the years that have followed, Rob has conducted investigations at some of the North East's most haunted locations, including Hylton Castle, Woodhorn Church, Flodden Field, Chillingham Castle, and the Castle Keep.

Rob's first book, *Ghostly Northumberland*, was published in 2008, and was followed by *Ghostly Tyne and Wear* in 2009.

The fourth book in this series, *Ghostly Cumbria*, will be available in 2011.

Sources &c. Recommended Reading

Anderson, Maureen *Foul Deeds and Suspicious Deaths in and around Durham* (Wharncliffe Books, 2003)

Bath, Jo *Dancing with the Devil and Other True Tales of Northern Witchcraft* (Tyne Bridge Publishing, 2002)

Green, Nigel *Tough Times and Grisly Crimes: A History of Crime in Northumberland and County Durham* (Nigel Green Media, 2005)

Hallam, Jack *Ghosts of the North* (David & Charles, 1976)

Jones, Richard *Haunted Britain and Ireland* (New Holland Publishers, 2003)

Jones, Richard *Haunted Castles of Britain and Ireland* (New Holland Publishers, 2005)

Jones, Richard *Haunted Inns of Britain and Ireland* (New Holland Publishers, 2004)

Jones, Richard *Haunted Houses of Britain and Ireland* (New Holland Publishers, 2005)

Liddell, Tony *Otherworld North East – Ghosts and Hauntings Explored* (Tyne Bridge Publishing, 2004)

Linahan, Liz *The North of England Ghost Trail* (Constable, 1997)

Long, Peter *The Hidden Places of Northumberland and Durham* (Travel Publishing Ltd, 2008)

Ritson, Darren W. *Ghost Hunter* (Grosvenor House Publishing Ltd, 2006)

Robson, Alan *Grisly Trails and Ghostly Tales* (Virgin Books, 1992)

Robson, Alan *Nightmare on Your Street* (Virgin Books, 1993)

Tegner, Henry *Ghosts of the North Country* (Butler Publishing, 1991)

Warren, Melanie & Wells, Tony *Ghosts of the North* (Broadcast Book, 1995)

Whyman, Phil *Phil Whyman's Dead Haunted: Paranormal Encounters and Investigations* (New Holland Publishers, 2007)

Other titles published by The History Press

Ghostly Tyne & Wear

ROB KIRKUP

From reports of haunted castles, pubs, theatres and shopping arcades, to heart-stopping accounts of apparitions, poltergeists and related supernatural phenomena, *Ghostly Tyne & Wear* investigates thirty of the most haunted locations in Tyne & Wear today. Drawing on historical and contemporary sources, this selection includes a phantom highwayman at Blacksmith's Table Restaurant in Washington, a Carry On film legend who haunts the Empire Theatre in Sunderland and a mischievous poltergeist at the Central Arcade in Newcastle-upon-Tyne.

978 0 7509 5109 8

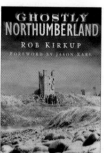

Ghostly Northumberland

ROB KIRKUP

Ghostly Northumberland investigates twenty of the most haunted locations in Northumberland. This work includes a piano-playing ghost at Bamburgh Castle, the White Lady of Cresswell Tower, a mischievous poltergeist at the Schooner Hotel, as well as sightings of torturer John Sage, who continues to stalk the dungeons at Chillingham Castle.

978 0 7509 5043 5

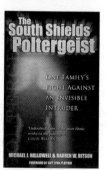

The South Shields Poltergeist:
One Family's Fight Against an Invisible Intruder

MICHAEL J. HALLOWELL & DARREN W. RITSON

In December 2005 a family began to experience poltergeist-like phenomena in their home. Slowly but steadily the phenomena escalated, and in July 2006 the authors were asked to investigate. This book is a chilling diary of an ongoing poltergeist case which the authors believe rivals any previously documented.

978 0 7524 5274 6

Paranormal Newcastle

GORDON RUTTER

With almost 2,000 years of continuous habitation, the city of Newcastle boasts a long history of paranormal occurrences. This richly illustrated book covers a fascinating range of strange events. From UFO sightings before the First World War, holy healing wells and bleeding statues, to puma sightings, ghosts, poltergeists and other bizarre apparitions, this incredible volume will invite the reader to view the city in a whole new light.

978 0 7524 4917 3

Visit our website and discover thousands of other History Press books.

www.thehistorypress.co.uk